Microeconomics

Louis Kaplow
Finn M. W. Caspersen and Household International Professor of Law and Economics Harvard University

Steven Shavell
Samuel R. Rosenthal Professor of Law and Economics Director, John M. Olin Center for Law, Economics, and Business Harvard University

Reprinted from
Analytical Methods for Lawyers

© 2004 By FOUNDATION PRESS

       395 Hudson Street

       New York, NY 10014

       Phone Toll Free 1–877–888–1330

       Fax (212) 367–6799

       fdpress.com

Printed in the United States of America

ISBN 1–58778–816–0

TEXT IS PRINTED ON 10% POST CONSUMER RECYCLED PAPER

Preface

This short book is a self-contained and reader-friendly primer on the subject of microeconomics. The book can serve either as an introduction to microeconomics or as a review for a person who once took a course in it. The book covers the basic areas of microeconomics: supply and demand and the determination of prices and quantities in competitive markets, problems with markets (imperfect information, monopoly, and externalities), public goods, and welfare economics. The book is drawn from the Foundation Press textbook *Analytical Methods for Lawyers* and should be useful for any person (lawyer or not) who wants to learn about microeconomics.

Cambridge, Massachusetts
August 2004

Contents

1. Introduction

Microeconomics is the branch of economics that focuses on the behavior of individual actors and that deals with individual markets. In contrast, *macroeconomics* analyzes broad economic phenomena — the overall level of economic activity, unemployment, interest rates, inflation, and the like. Our survey of microeconomics will begin with the classical theory of a competitive market. Then we'll move on to imperfect consumer information, monopoly and imperfect competition, externalities, public goods, and welfare economics. In doing so, we'll cover much of what is traditionally addressed in a course on microeconomics, although more compactly.

2. The Theory of the Competitive Market

How are the price and the quantity of goods sold on a market determined? In what sense can the price and the quantity be evaluated as socially good or bad? These are classic questions, and we will consider them in this section assuming that markets are competitive.

There are various ways of describing what is meant by a *competitive market*. A rough description is simply this: each consumer and each seller essentially take the prevailing price as given, because each individual is a small actor in the market in the sense that each person's transactions are a tiny fraction of all transactions. This is a good approximation to the truth in many markets, such as those for generic commodities like wheat and steel, and it is nearly true for a host of goods that aren't quite generic, like pizza and refrigerators. Even sellers of many branded products, like Starbucks coffee, can't sell very much if they deviate too greatly from the prevailing price for their type of product; thus, for some purposes, we can regard these products as being sold in a more or less competitive market. One way of describing a firm in a competitive market is to say that it is a price *taker*, as opposed to a price *maker*.

Price and total quantity sold in a competitive market are determined through the interaction of two forces: supply and demand. These twin forces are encapsulated in the notions of supply curves and demand curves. We will focus on each type of curve individually, and then we'll look at how, together, they can be used to find the price of an item and the quantity sold in a market.

A. Demand Curves

A *demand curve* for strawberries is shown in Figure 1. It records the total quantity of strawberries that people would want to purchase, depending on the price. The demand curve doesn't indicate the quantity of strawberries that people actually want to purchase. Rather, it is a *hypothetical* registering of the total quantity that they would want to buy at different possible prices. We can see from the curve that, at the price of $1.00 per quart, the total quantity of strawberries that people would wish to buy is 110,000 quarts; at $2.00 per quart, 60,000 quarts; at $3.00 per quart, 10,000 quarts; and so forth.

The total demand for a good falls as its price rises because, of course, people often decide to do without it, buy less of it, or perhaps substitute another good for it. When the price of strawberries rises, people may decide to skip putting fruit in their breakfast cereal, put fewer strawberries in their cereal, or substitute bananas or raisins for strawberries in their cereal. This, then, is why the total amount that people want to buy goes down as the price goes up, or, equivalently, why the total amount that people want to buy goes up as the price goes down. The graphical implication of this point is that demand curves generally slope downward.

The demand curve can be conceived of as reflecting the demand for a good by a named, relevant population of individuals — for example, all the people in a city, state, or country, or everybody in the world — or by single individual. Usually, what the demand curve is representing is stated or is clear from context.

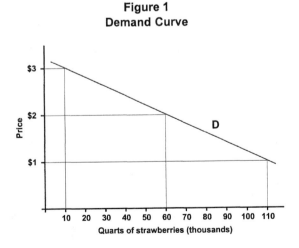

Figure 1
Demand Curve

It's worth noting that the graph of demand is drawn with quantity represented on the horizontal axis and price on the vertical axis. This is merely a convention; there is no logical reason why it has to be drawn this way.

1. Shift in the demand curve. When something affects the entire relationship between price and total quantity demanded, the demand curve shifts. Suppose, for example, that there's a scare about strawberries raised, perhaps by news reports that some strawberries are contaminated with a bacterium that can cause illness. We would expect the total quantity demanded to go down: at any given price, people would want to buy fewer strawberries — perhaps far fewer. As can be seen in Figure 2, the result would

---

Box 1
Where Do Demand Curves Come From?

Economists have a wealth of data that they use to estimate demand curves. The general way this is done is to look at how the demand for a good varies as its price has actually varied. Prices for most goods change over time, and economists can see how the total amount purchased has fluctuated with changes in price. Also, prices tend to vary somewhat at any given time, depending on location of sale. Of course, there are many reasons that quantity purchased will change other than that the price changed. For instance, suppose that incomes of people go up at the same time that the price of foreign travel falls, and that the amount of foreign travel increases. Might this increase in travel be due more to the income increase than to the fall in price? Fortunately, given enough data and statistical tools, the effects of factors like income on amount purchased can be disentangled from the effect of price, and a demand curve can be obtained.

be a leftward shift in the curve. At any given price, the total amount demanded would be lower than it was originally — for example, at $2.00 per quart, instead of being 60,000 quarts, it would be only 30,000 quarts.

Such a *shift* in the demand curve is sometimes distinguished from a movement *along* a *given* demand curve, which is to say, a movement from one quantity demanded at a particular price to another quantity demanded at another price. Let's look again at the old demand curve in Figure 1 (the demand curve for strawberries before the news about bacterial contamination). At a price of $2.00, the demand for strawberries is 60,000 quarts, and at a price of $3.00, it's 10,000 quarts. The change in demand from 60,000 quarts to 10,000 quarts would be described as a movement along the demand curve due to a price change.

Figure 3 shows the consequence of something that would increase the total quantity of strawberries demanded — for example, a report from the National Institutes of Health that strawberries increase longevity and reduce the risk of cancer. The demand curve to the right of the original one shows that, at any price, the total amount that people would demand is higher than it had been initially.

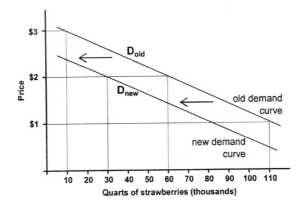

Figure 2
Leftward Shift in the Demand Curve

Figure 3
Rightward Shift in the Demand Curve

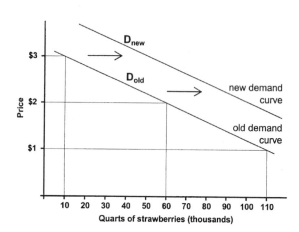

Demand curves can shift when any factor affecting the amount that people would want to buy comes into play. One such factor is individual income. (What would you expect to happen to the demand curve for strawberries if incomes rose?) Another general factor affecting the demand curve for a good is the price of substitute goods. (What would you expect to happen to the demand curve for strawberries if the price of bananas increased?) A related factor is the price of complementary goods. (What would you expect to happen to the demand curve for strawberries if the price of breakfast cereal fell?)

2. The demand curve and the concept of price elasticity. The slope of a demand curve reflects the responsiveness of quantity demanded to price. From Figure 4A, we can see that a demand curve that slopes very steeply signifies that the amount people would buy is *not* much affected by a change in price. When price doubles from $1.00 to $2.00, for instance, the quantity that people would want to purchase falls only from 100 to 90. Contrast this with the less steep demand curve in Figure 4B, which shows that a doubling in price from $1.00 to $2.00 would result in a large decrease in quantity demanded, from 180 down to 40.

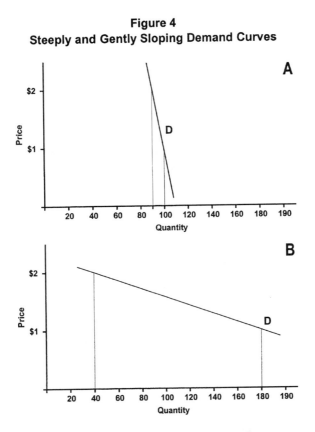

Figure 4
Steeply and Gently Sloping Demand Curves

Economists use a special number — the *price elasticity of demand* — to capture the degree of responsiveness of total quantity demanded to changes in the price of a good. It is defined this way:

$$\text{price elasticity of demand} = \frac{\%\ \text{change in quantity demanded}}{\%\ \text{change in price}}$$

To illustrate, let's return to the steep demand curve of Figure 4A we just looked at. According to this curve, when the price goes from $1.00 to $2.00, the quantity demanded falls from 100 to 90. Thus, the percent change in price is 100% (from $1.00 to $2.00), and the percent change in quantity is 10% (from 100 to 90), so the price elasticity is 10%/100%, or .1.[1] In the case of the less steep demand curve in Figure 4B, when the price goes from $1.00 to $2.00, the quantity demanded falls from 180 to 40. Thus, the percent change in price is 100%, and the percent change in quantity is 78% (i.e., 140/180), so the price elasticity is 78%/100%, which equals 0.78. Let's work through just one more example. Suppose that the price of some good falls from $5.00 to $4.00 and the total quantity demanded rises from 200 units to 300 units. In this case, the percent change in price is 20%, and the percent change in quantity is 50%, so the elasticity is 2.5 (i.e., 50%/20% = 2.5). Evidently, then, higher elasticity numbers correspond to greater responsiveness of quantity to price. If the elasticity is greater than 1.0, the demand relationship is said to be elastic, and if the elas-

Table 1
Common Demand Elasticities

Product	Price elasticity of demand
Coffee	0.3
Cigarettes	0.3
Shoes	0.7
Automobiles	1.2
Foreign travel	1.8
Restaurant meals	2.3
Motion pictures	3.7

Source: Arthur O'Sullivan and Steven M. Sheffrin, *Microeconomics* (Prentice Hall, 1998), page 84.

---

1. In computing the percent change, one convention — which will be ours — is to use the beginning number as the base. Thus, when the price changes from $1.00 to $2.00, we use $1.00 as the base, and since the change is $1.00, the percent change is $1.00/$1.00, or 100%.

ticity is less than 1.0, the demand relationship is said to be *inelastic.*[2] Some elasticities of demand are shown in Table 1.

With elasticity figures like this, which economists have estimated statistically, the effect of price changes on the amount sold can be readily calculated. For example, what would you predict to be the effect on cigarette purchases of a doubling in price (perhaps as a result of a hefty increase in cigarette taxes)? The percent change in price would be 100%, and, according to the table, the elasticity of demand for cigarettes is 0.3. Given that 0.3 would be the percent change in quantity divided by 100%, the percent change in quantity would be 30%. Hence, cigarette demand should fall by 30%.

Optional material

Technical points. Two technical points should be noted about price elasticity of demand. First, because an *increase* in price results in a *decline* in quantity demanded, one percentage is positive and the other is negative, so their ratio is literally a *negative* number. Although price elasticities are sometimes reported as negative numbers, more often the convention of ignoring the minus sign is followed, and that's what we do here. This is confusing, admittedly, but it's something you should be aware of.

Second, although we have spoken of *the* price elasticity, it is not necessarily a fixed value. Its value may well depend on the prices and quantities at which we begin and end on the demand curve, as becomes apparent when we do some

---

2. You might ask yourself why economists defined elasticity as they did. In particular, why don't economists simply use the slope of a demand curve as a measure of the responsiveness of quantity demanded to price and call this the elasticity? The reason is that tricks can be played with the slope of a curve. For example, the slope of a curve can always be made to be steep by choosing to use large quantity units (e.g., by measuring strawberries in tons instead of quarts). In contrast, if elasticity is defined as economists have chosen, the elasticity for a price change remains the same regardless of the units in which quantities and prices are measured.

calculations. If we begin and end on a fairly flat region of a demand curve, the calculated elasticity would tend to be high, whereas if both points are on a steep region of the curve, elasticity would be low. Hence, elasticity is really not a fixed number, and it's often treated and spoken of as an approximation.

Price elasticity and revenue. There is a relationship between elasticity and the responsiveness of revenue (i.e., price × quantity) to price. First, if the elasticity is greater than 1.0, then an increase in price reduces revenue. Let's suppose that the elasticity is 2.0 and that, when the price is $2.00, the quantity sold is 300. In this case, revenue is $600.00. Then let's suppose that the price goes up to $2.20, which is a 10% increase. Because the elasticity is 2.0, we know that quantity must fall by 20%, to 240 (because 20% × 300 = 60). Hence, revenue is $2.20 × 240.00, or $528.00. That is, revenue falls. This makes sense intuitively: if quantity is very responsive to price, then when price goes up, the fall in quantity will be more important than the increase in price, and the quantity reaction will drag down revenue. Likewise, a decrease in price will raise revenue.

Similar logic (which we won't go into here) shows that when elasticity is less than 1.0, an increase in price will raise revenue, and a decrease in price will lower revenue.

Other types of elasticities of demand. There are other concepts of elasticity. The *cross elasticity of demand* for a good is the responsiveness of the demand for the good to a change in the price of *another* good. For instance, the cross elasticity of demand for strawberries with respect to bananas is the responsiveness of the quantity demanded of strawberries to a change in the price of bananas. If bananas become more expensive, we would expect some people to switch from bananas to strawberries and thus the demand for strawberries to increase. Formally, cross elasticity is defined as follows:

$$\text{cross elasticity of demand} = \frac{\%\ \text{change in quantity demanded}}{\%\ \text{change in price of another good}}$$

So, if the cross elasticity of demand for strawberries with respect to bananas is 0.2 and the price of bananas goes up by 50% for some reason, the quantity of strawberries demanded should rise by 10% (i.e., 0.2 × 50% = 10%). A high cross elasticity signifies that goods are pretty substitutable in consumers' eyes. If we want to know how substitutable two different branded products are — say, BMWs and Mercedes — we would look at the cross elasticity of demand between them. (Do you think that the cross elasticity of demand for BMWs with respect to the price of Mercedes is higher or lower than the cross elasticity of demand for BMWs with respect to the price of the Ford Taurus?)

Income elasticity is a measure of the responsiveness of quantity demanded to changes in individuals' income (rather than to the price of a good). Specifically,

$$\text{income elasticity of demand} = \frac{\%\text{ change in quantity demanded}}{\%\text{ change in income}}$$

For example, if the income elasticity of demand for laptop computers is 1.5 and we learn that incomes have risen by 6%, we would expect the demand for laptops to go up by 9% (i.e., 1.5 × 6% = 9%).

B. Supply Curves

The *supply curve* is a graph of the total quantity that firms in an industry would be willing to sell at different possible prices. According to the supply curve for strawberries in Figure 5, when the price rises from $2.00 to $3.00, the quantity of strawberries that firms want to sell increases from 60,000 quarts to 90,000 quarts.

Why should firms want to sell more strawberries when the price goes up? There are two basic reasons: (1) Existing firms in the strawberry industry will tend to produce more strawberries if they can sell them at a higher price. They will do so because they will invest in equipment that will more efficiently handle strawberries, thereby reducing crushing and wastage; because they will plant more land with strawberries; and so forth. (2) Over time, new firms will enter the industry. For example, farms that had

Figure 5
Supply Curve

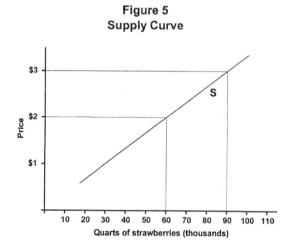

Quarts of strawberries (thousands)

devoted their efforts to other crops may switch to strawberries, and perhaps some individuals who are not growing any crops will enter the strawberry industry.[3]

How much the supply of strawberries will rise when the price increases will depend on the joint effects on existing firms and new entrants.

A point that deserves to be emphasized is that the effect that a change in price has on the quantity supplied by an industry depends, importantly, on the length of time in question. Economists often speak of the *short run* — by which they mean a period too short for new firms to be able to enter the market and too short also for existing firms to be to able make major changes in capital and equipment. Over the *long run,* however, both of these things can happen. Thus, the short-run supply curve is steeper than the long-run supply curve. (Can you explain why?)

1. Shift in the supply curve. A shift in the supply curve is analogous to a shift in the demand curve. It occurs when something affects the relationship between price and quantity supplied. Sup-

---

3. Note that, if the price of strawberries falls, existing firms may exit from the industry.

Figure 6
Leftward Shift in the Supply Curve

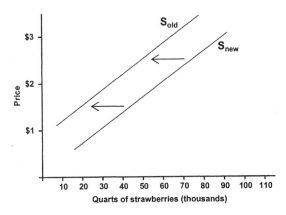

pose that a fungus attacks strawberries and that, as a result, they become harder to grow to maturity. The quantity of strawberries produced at any given price will tend to fall, as illustrated in Figure 6 by the leftward shift in the supply curve. Or suppose that a genetically engineered strawberry resistant to disease and rot is developed. In this case, the quantity of strawberries that firms supply at any given price will be likely to rise, and the supply curve will shift to the right, as depicted in Figure 7.

Figure 7
Rightward Shift in the Supply Curve

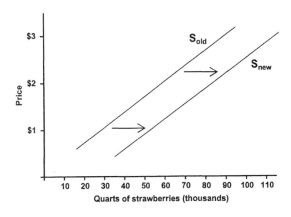

2. The supply curve and elasticity of supply. The concept of elasticity of supply is similar to that of elasticity of demand, so the discussion can be brief here. Observe first that a steeply rising supply curve, as in Figure 8A, corresponds to a good for which an increase in price results in only a small change in quantity produced. The interpretation, therefore, is that existing firms won't produce much more when price goes up because they can't profitably do so and also that new firms won't enter the market in significant numbers. Indeed, an almost vertical supply curve signifies that, for the good in question, an increase in price would result in virtually no increase in quantity produced. An example of such a good is land: when the price goes up, more cannot be produced (short of draining swamps and the like).

Second, note that a fairly flat demand curve, such as the one in Figure 8B, corresponds to a good for which a small increase in price results in a large increase in quantity supplied. One interpretation is that existing firms will produce much more when price goes up by a little. This would be the case when a lot more of a good can be produced if only a modest amount more would need to be spent per unit — for instance, by spending slightly more on labor or materials. Another interpretation is that, if the price goes up slightly, many new firms will enter the industry. This

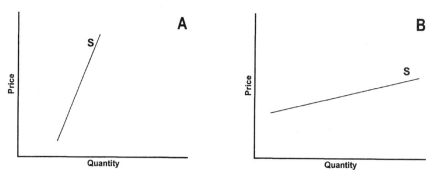

Figure 8
Steeply and Gently Sloping Supply Curves

could happen if the production technology is fairly widely known and access to material inputs and labor is nearly equal.

Supply elasticity is formally defined this way:

$$\text{elasticity of supply} = \frac{\% \text{ change in quantity supplied}}{\% \text{ change in price}}$$

To illustrate, suppose that the supply elasticity is 2.0 and that the price rises by 10%. The amount supplied by the industry would increase by 20%.

C. Determination of Market Price and Quantity

1. Intersection of /supply and demand curves determines equilibrium price and quantity. We can predict what will occur in a competitive market — what the price and the quantity will be — by using supply and demand curves. *The price and the quantity would be expected to gravitate toward the price and quantity at which the supply and demand curves intersect.*

Consider Figure 9, in which the demand and supply curves for strawberries intersect where the price is $2.00 per quart and the quantity supplied is 60,000 quarts. Let's analyze why the point of intersection of these two curves determines the price and quantity that we expect to observe.

Figure 9
Demand and Supply Curves and Market Equilibrium

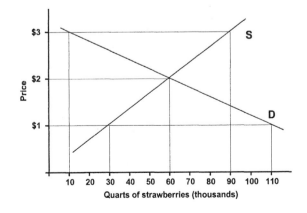

When the price of strawberries is $2.00 per quart, people want to buy 60,000 quarts, and industry also wants to produce 60,000 quarts. In other words, the total quantity that people want to buy *matches* the total quantity that industry wants to produce. Thus, the situation is one in which there is a balance, or an *equilibrium,* between consumers' desire to purchase and industry's willingness to produce.

Moreover, any price different from $2.00 per quart (the price at which the demand and supply curves intersect) cannot persist. To explain: Suppose that the price is above $2.00 for some reason — say, at $3.00 per quart. We can see from the supply curve that, for the price to remain at this higher-than-equilibrium level, industry would supply a larger quantity, namely, 90,000 quarts rather than 60,000 quarts. But the demand curve tells us that, at $3.00 per quart, people would purchase only 10,000 quarts. Hence, the quantity of strawberries brought to stores and put onto shelves — 90,000 quarts — would far exceed the quantity that people would buy — 10,000 quarts. Such a situation is often referred to as one of excess supply. Obviously, it cannot persist — because when stores find that they have strawberries on hand that aren't selling, they *lower the price* in order to sell more strawberries. (This would be so even if strawberries weren't perishable, for stores wouldn't want to store a commodity forever.) The foregoing argument applies whenever price exceeds $2.00, because at any such price the quantity supplied would be above 60,000 quarts and the quantity demanded would be below 60,000 quarts; thus, there would always be an excess supply and a downward pressure on price. Our conclusion, therefore, is that no price exceeding $2.00 can persist and that price must fall if it exceeds $2.00.

Now suppose that the price is below $2.00 per quart — say, at $1.00 per quart. Industry would produce 30,000 quarts, whereas people would want to purchase 110,000 quarts. In this situation the quantity demanded would outstrip the quantity produced. It is a situation of *excess demand,* and it would result in an *upward movement of price.* In particular, sellers would notice that they were running short of strawberries and would, naturally, start raising prices. Hence, a situation in which the price is $1.00 could not persist. In fact, any price below $2.00 would lead to an upward pressure on price.

Obviously, if at any price above $2.00 the price would fall and if at any price below $2.00 the price would rise, the price would gravitate toward $2.00. Moreover, we would expect the price to stick at $2.00 once it got there. Recall that at $2.00 per quart the total quantity that people would want to buy is 60,000 quarts, which is also the quantity that industry would want to produce. Hence, there would neither be a shortage of strawberries, resulting in an upward pressure on price, nor a surfeit of strawberries, resulting in a downward pressure on price. Hence, the price of $2.00 per quart would indeed be stable. This is another reason why it is called the equilibrium price.

Corresponding to the $2.00 equilibrium price, where the supply and demand curves intersect, is a quantity that is both produced and demanded — namely, 60,000 quarts. This is the *equilibrium quantity.*

2. Changes in equilibrium with changes in demand and supply curves. If the demand curve or the supply curve changes, the equilibrium price and quantity generally change as well. For example, let's say that strawberries are found to have previously unknown health benefits and that, in response to this good health news, the demand curve shifts to the right. As we can see from Figure 10, the point of intersection of the supply and demand curves would change from point A to point B. In other words, the equilibrium price and the quantity sold would increase: the price would rise from $2.00 to $2.50, and the quantity sold would go from 60,000 quarts to 75,000 quarts. A story can be told to explain how this would happen: As we can see in Figure 10, if stores didn't react to the good news about strawberries and didn't raise the price, there would be a shortage of strawberries. The total quantity demanded would increase from 60,000 quarts at a price

Figure 10
Effect of a Shift in the Demand Curve on Equilibrium

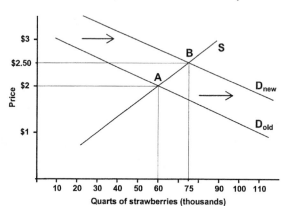

Quarts of strawberries (thousands)

of $2.00 to about 100,000 quarts. (Make sure you can see from the graph that, according to the new demand curve, approximately 100,000 quarts would be demanded at the price of $2.00.) This shortage of strawberries would lead to an increase in the price. An increase in price from $2.00 would have two effects. On one hand, the quantity of strawberries demanded by consumers would fall from the 100,000-quart level to a lower level (moving along the new demand curve). On the other hand, the quantity of strawberries produced would rise from the 60,000-quart level. When the price reached $2.50, the amount demanded would have shrunk from 100,000 quarts to 75,000 quarts, and the amount supplied would have grown from 60,000 quarts to 75,000 quarts. In other words, there would be a new equilibrium at the higher price and higher quantity.

Figure 11 illustrates the effect of an increase, a rightward shift, in the supply curve following, say, a decrease in the cost of producing strawberries due to lower labor costs. Can you tell a story explaining why the new equilibrium price would be $1.50 per quart and the new quantity sold would be 85,000 quarts?

Figure 11
Effect of a Shift in the Supply Curve on Equilibrium

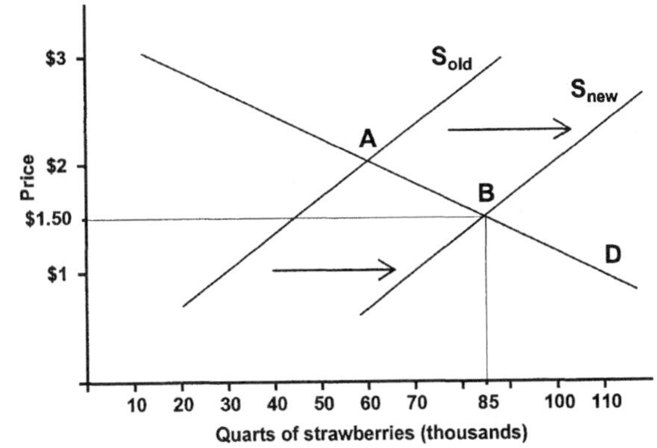

D. Government Intervention in Markets

We can use demand and supply curves to understand various kinds of government policies involving market intervention. Let's consider three.

1. Price floors. A classic government policy is to place a floor — that is, a minimum — on the price of a good, such as a floor on the price of milk to help dairy farmers. The effect of a price floor can be seen in Figure 12.

Figure 12
Price Floor

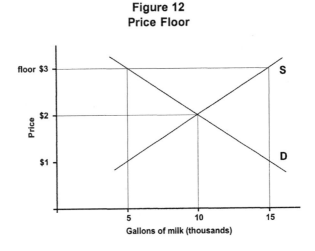

Box 2
Subsidies

Government can help producers like dairy farmers not by setting a price floor, but instead by *subsidizing* milk production. That is, the government can pay dairy farmers some amount per gallon of milk the farmers sell on the market. How would you represent a subsidy using demand and supply curves? (Hint: look a bit ahead at a commodity tax and note that a subsidy is like a tax, except it's in the opposite direction.) Verify that the effect of a subsidy would be to increase the quantity of milk produced. What would the effect of it be on the market price? How does it compare to a price floor?

As illustrated, were there no price floor, milk would sell at an equilibrium price of $2.00 per gallon, and 10,000 gallons would be produced and sold. Given a price floor of $3.00 per gallon, the quantity demanded would fall to 5,000 gallons, and this is all that would be sold. However, at a price of $3.00 per gallon, the dairy industry would be willing to produce 15,000 gallons, even though they would learn that only 5,000 gallons would be purchased. This situation, in which industry would want to produce more milk than people would want to buy could not result in a decline in the price of milk, because the assumption is that government has set a floor of $3.00 per gallon. Hence, some mechanism has to be devised, by government or by dairy farmers, to determine which farmers enjoy the privilege of selling milk at $3.00 per gallon. The mechanism might be an allocation system, whereby each dairy farmer is allowed to sell a certain number of gallons of milk (perhaps based on past sales).

2. Price ceilings. Now let's consider a government policy of the opposite type, in which a ceiling — a maximum — is placed on a price, say, to protect consumers against high prices. Suppose, for instance, that a ceiling were imposed on the price of heating oil. Consider the graphical representation of such a price control in Figure 13, where the equilibrium price of heating oil is $2.00 per gallon and the number of gallons supplied is 10,000. If a price ceiling were put into effect to limit the price to $1.00 per gallon, the demand for heating oil would be 15,000 gallons, whereas the number of gallons supplied by industry would be lower, only 5,000 gallons. This is a situation of excess demand: the amount of heating oil that people would want to buy would exceed by 10,000 gallons the amount that industry supplies. Somehow, the 5,000 gallons of heating oil supplied has to be distributed among people, perhaps by means of an allocation based on size of buildings, perhaps by some other means.

3. Commodity taxes. Now let's consider a classic commodity tax, such as a tax of $1.00 per bottle of perfume. When people have to pay an extra dollar for a bottle of perfume, the demand at any given market price should fall, and the demand curve should shift to the left. The price, then, should fall, and so should the quantity. Such a scenario is illustrated in Figure 14: the equilibrium price decreases from $3.00 per bottle to $2.50 per bottle (but the after-tax price is $3.50 per bottle), and the equilibrium quan-

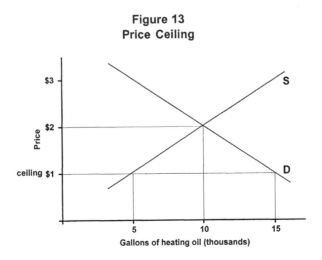

Figure 13
Price Ceiling

Figure 14
Commodity Tax

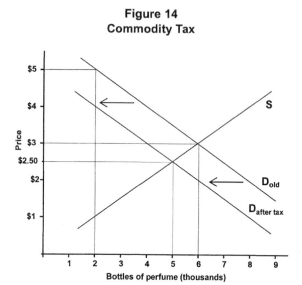

Bottles of perfume (thousands)

tity goes from 6,000 bottles down to 5,000 bottles. Note that the after-tax demand curve is vertically below the old demand curve by a distance of exactly $1.00. We can understand why by considering any price and the corresponding quantity on the old demand curve in Figure 14 let's say $5.00 and 2,000 bottles. If people had to pay $5.00, they would buy 2,000 bottles. However, at a market price of $4.00 ($1.00 less than the original) *plus* a tax of $1.00, the after-tax, total price of a bottle would be $5.00. So people would be expected to buy precisely 2,000 bottles if the market price were $4.00 and a tax of $1.00 were levied. Additionally, we can tell from the geometry of the supply and demand curves — again, see Figure 6-14 — that the market price can't fall by as much as the $1.00 tax; it must fall by less. (Can you explain why this is so in intuitive terms?)

E. Social Welfare and the Market

We have seen how price and quantity are determined in competitive markets and how various policies affect price and quantity, but we haven't yet evaluated the social desirability of price and quantity outcomes. Although we won't focus on the general topic of social welfare until later, we should be familiar with one measure of social welfare, a simple and intuitively appealing one, at this point: *the value that parties obtain from consuming goods minus the cost of producing them.* This quantity is sometimes called *total surplus,* or just surplus, because it's the excess of the value placed on things over the cost of making them. The appeal of surplus as a social goal or measuring rod is that it reflects in a positive way the value that we assign to things and in a negative way the resources needed to produce them. Despite the drawbacks associated with measuring social welfare in this way (we'll discuss them later), it is a very useful tool for thinking, and economists frequently employ it as a benchmark for evaluating policies.

1. Value of consumption. The value an individual obtains from consumption is conventionally measured as the maximum a person is willing to pay for the item consumed. For example, if I'm willing to pay as much as $5.00 for a quart of strawberries, then $5.00 is the measure of my valuation. In fact, it measures my valuation in at least two senses: (1) My valuation is not greater than $5.00 — say, for example, $6.00 — because if it were, then this higher amount — $6.00 — would be the maximum I am willing to pay for the strawberries, but in fact I'm not willing to pay more than $5.00. (2) My valuation is not less than $5.00 — say, $4.00 — because if it were, then this lower amount — $4.00 — would be the maximum I'm willing to pay, whereas I'm actually willing to pay as much as $5.00 for the strawberries.

Table 2
Valuations of Individuals

Individual	Value placed on 1 quart of strawberries
Amy	$5.00
Bob	$4.00
Ralph	$3.00
Jill	$2.00

Figure 15
Demand Curve

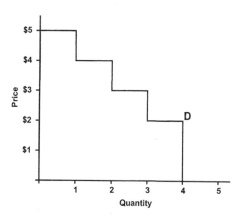

Similarly, *total value* reflects the sum of valuations assigned by all of the individuals in a group. Suppose, for example, that four individuals assign four different values to a quart of strawberries (see Table 2), and assume, for the sake of simplicity, that none of them wants more than a quart. If 4 quarts are consumed, 1 quart by each person, the total value enjoyed is $5.00 + $4.00 + $3.00 + $2.00 = $14.00.

To see how we can use a demand curve to get information about total value placed on consumption, let's look at Figure 15, the demand curve for strawberries representing the same four individuals as above. Note that, at a price of $5.00 per quart, only Amy would buy strawberries, so the quantity demanded would be 1 quart. At $4.00 per quart, both Amy and Bob would purchase a quart, so the quantity demanded would be 2 quarts. And so forth. If we look closely at the curve, a very important point becomes apparent: at any price at which strawberries are sold, *the total value placed on the quantity purchased equals the area under the demand curve* up to that quantity.

For example, at a price of $5.00, at which just Amy purchases a quart of strawberries, the area under the demand curve is $5.00 (i.e., 1 × $5.00 = $5.00), which is Amy's willingness to pay for a quart. If the price is $4.00, the demand is for 2 quarts, so the area under the demand curve up to 2 quarts is $9.00 (i.e., 1 × $5.00 + 1 × $4.00 = $9.00). This is the total value placed by the two people, Amy and Bob, who would purchase the 2 quarts. We could continue in like manner to calculate total value at other prices. Clearly, the area under the demand curve, up to the quantity demanded at any given price, equals the total value assigned by all the people who would make purchases at that price. To look at one more example, the area under the demand curve up to 3 quarts (as designated by the shaded region in Figure 16) is the total value placed by Amy, Bob, and Ralph if strawberries sold at $3.00 per quart: 1 × $5.00 + 1 × $4.00 + 1 × $3.00 = $12.00.

Although the preceding examples involved purchases of the same quantity, 1 quart, by each of several people, the approach is the same when one person buys different quantities, depending on the price. Suppose, for instance, that Lucy places a value of $5.00 on having 1 quart of strawberries, an additional value of $4.00 on having a second quart, an additional value of $3.00 on having a third quart, and yet an additional value of $2.00 on having a fourth quart. The demand curve representing the total value placed on strawberries by Lucy alone — that is, one person — would be identical to the demand curve in Figure 15. To look at

Figure 16
Area under the Demand Curve

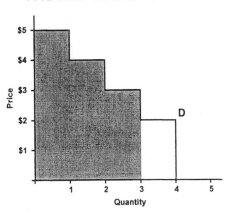

this situation from a slightly different perspective: at a price of $4.00, Lucy would buy 2 quarts, because the first and second quarts would each be worth at least $4.00 to her, but she wouldn't buy a third quart at $4.00, because its value to her would be only $3.00. Also, by the same logic given above, the area under the demand curve at any given quantity of strawberries would equal the total value that Lucy places on that quantity.

2. **Consumer surplus.** The difference between the value consumers place on what they buy and the price they actually pay is referred to as *consumer surplus*. For instance, if the price of strawberries is $3.00, and Amy buys a quart that she values at $5.00, her consumer surplus is $2.00 (i.e., $5.00 − $3.00 = $2.00). It is a measure of her benefit after she has paid for the quart of strawberries. Like total valuation, total consumer surplus can be easily seen from the demand curve. Let's consider again the demand curve for strawberries that we've been working with. At a price of $3.00, Amy, Bob, and Ralph purchase a quart each. Amy's consumer surplus is $2.00 (i.e., $5.00 − $3.00 = $2.00), which corresponds to the area between the demand curve and the $3.00 price line (see Figure 17). Bob's consumer surplus is $1.00 (i.e., $4.00 − $3.00 = $1.00), again the area between the demand curve and the price line. Ralph's consumer surplus is zero, as the

Figure 17
Consumer Surplus

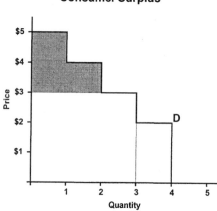

amount he pays is exactly equal to the value he places on strawberries. The total surplus for these three people is, therefore, $3.00 (i.e., $2.00 + $1.00 = $3.00). In this example, then, and in general, *total consumer surplus corresponds to the area between the price line and the demand curve.* To put it differently: the area under the entire demand curve is the total value (as we already know), and the area under the price line is the total amount paid by consumers for the quantity they purchase, so the difference must be the surplus they enjoy.

Obviously, for many of the things that we buy, we enjoy substantial consumer surplus, for the prices we pay for them are much lower than what we would be willing to pay.

3. Production cost. Before we can determine total surplus, we have to consider the cost of producing goods. As it turns out, total production costs equal the *area under the supply curve.* The reason why this is so is analogous to the reason why the area under the demand curve equals total consumer valuation. We can see this by extending our hypothetical strawberry scenario. Let's say that four firms produce strawberries and that each produces exactly 1 quart. (Admittedly, no firm would produce just 1 quart, but we make this assumption for expositional convenience.) Let's also say that each firm faces a different production cost (see Table 3). With this information at hand, we can construct the supply curve (see Figure 18): At a price of $1.00 per quart, only one firm, Alpha, would produce strawberries, so the total quantity produced would be 1 quart. If strawberries sold for $2.00 per quart, 2 quarts would be produced, because two firms, Alpha and

Table 3
Production Costs of Firms

Firm	Production cost for 1 quart of strawberries
Alpha	$1.00
Beta	$2.00
Gamma	$3.00
Delta	$4.00

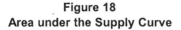

Figure 18
Area under the Supply Curve

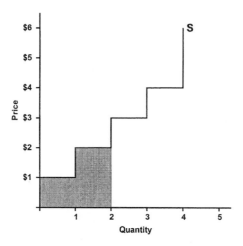

Beta, would produce 1 quart each. And so forth for prices of $3.00 and $4.00. Now it's easy to verify that the area under the supply curve up to the quantity produced is a measure of the total production cost: at a price of $2.00, the area under the curve (i.e., the

Figure 19
Profit

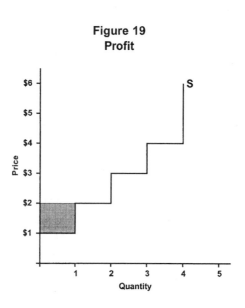

Box 3
Ticket Scalping and Surplus

Some people – so-called scalpers — buy tickets to events, like baseball games, and then sell them to people who come to the events. This would appear to increase surplus: people who buy tickets from scalpers benefit – they save the time they'd have to spend waiting in line, or they get better tickets than they otherwise would – and the scalpers make money from the transactions. Yet ticket scalping is often illegal. Why should that be?

---

shaded area in Figure 18) is $3.00 (i.e., $1.00 + $2.00 = $3.00), which is Alpha's and Beta's combined costs of production.

4. Profit, or producer surplus. In a similar way, we can determine a firm's profit from its supply curve. If the price is $2.00, Alpha makes a profit of $2.00 – $1.00, which is $1.00, and Beta a profit of $2.00 – $2.00, or $0.00 (i.e., Beta doesn't make a profit). Thus, *profit equals the area between the price line and the supply curve*, as represented by the shaded area in Figure 19. This makes sense, as the area under the price line is total revenue and the area un-

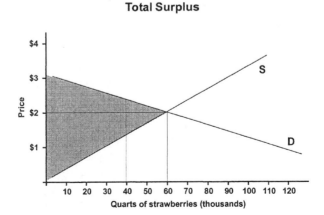

Figure 20
Total Surplus

der the supply curve measures total production cost. Sometimes profit is called *producer surplus*.

5. Surplus. Total surplus is, as we know, defined to be the difference between consumer valuation and production cost. With the aid of the demand and supply curves, we can figure it out for any quantity produced. Let's look at the demand and supply curves for strawberries in Figure 20. (We're now imagining many individuals and firms, whereas, for convenience, the preceding examples involved only a few.) For a quantity of 40,000 quarts, the value of the strawberries to consumers is the area under the demand curve up to 40,000 quarts, and the cost of producing them is the area under the supply curve up to 40,000 quarts. Hence, the surplus is the shaded area in between. More generally, then, *for any given quantity, surplus is the area between the demand and supply curves up to that quantity.*

6. Maximum surplus. It follows from what we've said that surplus can increase − that is, it is not at the maximum possible level − as long as quantity is less than the equilibrium quantity. Let's look again at the demand and supply curves for strawberries in Figure 20. When the quantity is to the left of the intersection of these two curves at 60,000 quarts, the demand curve is higher than the supply curve. This means that, if quantity is increased, the area between the two curves increases, so surplus rises. More directly, the value placed by some person on one additional quart of strawberries, as measured by the height of the demand curve, exceeds the cost of producing this quart; the quart should, therefore, be produced. When quantity reaches the equilibrium quantity, increasing production is no longer socially beneficial.

Similarly, surplus can always be increased if quantity exceeds the equilibrium quantity. As we can see from Figure 20, for any quantity to the right of 60,000 quarts, the supply curve is higher than the demand curve. In other words, beyond 60,000 quarts, production cost is higher than the value people place on strawberries; as a result, producing those quarts would reduce the surplus. By limiting production to 60,000 quarts, the savings from

Figure 21
Consumer Surplus and Profit

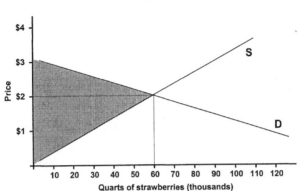

Quarts of strawberries (thousands)

not producing the additional quarts is greater than the amount by which people's valuations diminish; hence, surplus rises.

The conclusion, then, is that *surplus is maximized when quantity produced is the competitive equilibrium quantity.* In plain terms, the market will result in production of every unit whose cost is less than its value, but the market will not lead to production of any unit whose cost is greater than its value.

Graphically, the maximum surplus is reached when the market establishes the equilibrium price and the corresponding quantity is sold. At this price, the surplus is the shaded area in Figure 21. The upper shaded triangle is consumer surplus, and the lower shaded triangle is profit, or producer surplus. This should be geometrically obvious.[4]

We haven't yet explicitly noted the reason, as it is expressed in ordinary discourse, why competitive markets are good: through vigorous competition and unimpeded entry into an industry, prices fall and buyers are thereby made better off. This point can

---

4. The explanation may be expressed algebraically as well: Let v be the value of a unit of the good, c the production cost of that unit, and p the price of the good. Then the surplus created by production of that unit of the good is $v - c$, consumer surplus is $v - p$, and profit is $p - c$. But $v - c = (v - p) + (p - c)$; that is, surplus equals consumer surplus plus profit.

also be expressed in terms of surplus: lower prices resulting from competition and entry into an industry raise consumer surplus and thus surplus.[5]

7. Limitations of surplus as a measure of social welfare. Although surplus can be a useful measure of social welfare, it does have its limitations.

First, surplus represents an aggregate and doesn't reflect distributional factors. For example, surplus might be large overall but enjoyed mainly by rich individuals or, in the form of high profits, primarily by firms (though, ultimately, firms' profits are returned to the individuals who own the firms).

Second, surplus depends on the allocation of wealth in the population, because a person's willingness to pay for something (i.e., the measure of value used to calculate surplus) obviously depends on how much wealth the person has. For example, a larger surplus may be created by production of a sweater for a rich lady's poodle that she is more than willing to pay for than by production of a jar of peanut butter for a poor mother's hungry children that she is hesitant to pay for because of her lack of means.

Third, surplus as a measure of social welfare is based on the assumption that consumers properly appreciate the benefits of what they purchase. If they overestimate the value of goods, the willingness-to-pay measure exaggerates the real benefits of consumption; if they underestimate the value of goods, the willingness-to-pay measure understates the benefits of consumption. For example, if a good is of poor quality (such as a drug touted to prevent male-pattern baldness that doesn't do so) but people don't know this, they may be willing to pay a lot for it even though it won't actually produce the benefits they expect.

---

5. A more detailed explanation for why entry and competition raises surplus is that entry moves the supply curve to the right. Do you see why this must raise surplus, assuming that the quantity produced is the quantity at which the supply and demand curves intersect?

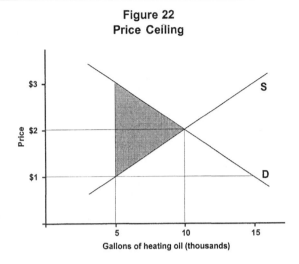

Figure 22
Price Ceiling

Despite these limitations — which can be addressed, however, as we will soon see — the notion of surplus is very useful, mainly because surplus is a rough proxy for social welfare. It corresponds to some sort of total "pie" that is society's to enjoy.

F. Social Welfare Evaluation of Government Intervention in Competitive Markets

We now have the tools and knowledge we need to be able to evaluate the reduction in social welfare, in terms of a decline in surplus, that accompanies certain government interventions in competitive markets. Let's look at two specific ones: price ceilings and taxes.

1. Price ceilings. The heating oil scenario we looked at earlier provides a good example. The graph from Figure 13 is reproduced, in slightly modified form (one area has been shaded), in Figure 22.

Because the price ceiling of $1.00 a gallon results in production and sale of only 5,000 gallons, whereas 10,000 gallons would be produced and sold at the equilibrium price of $2.00 per gallon, there is a loss in surplus relative to the maximum surplus. This loss is represented by the triangular area between the demand and supply curves from 5,000 gallons to 10,000 gallons. It is the forgone surplus due to the extra 5,000 gallons not being supplied.

This can be seen in a mechanical way: if 5,000 gallons are produced, surplus is the area between the demand and supply curves
up to the quantity of 5,000 gallons; and if the quantity is
10,000 gallons instead of 5,000 gallons, the area representing surplus expands to include the shaded area.

Intuitively, the price ceiling limits the surplus by effectively reducing the number of gallons supplied that cost less to produce
than people would be willing to pay for them. For instance, the
first 100 gallons or so beyond the 5,000th gallon would cost a bit
over $1.00 per gallon to produce (because the height of the supply
curve is just over $1.00 in this region), yet people value these gal-
lons at roughly $3.00 (because the height of the demand curve is
about at this level). Hence, because of the price ceiling, the people
who value the heating oil at almost $2.00 per gallon more than
production cost can't get it. (Note that although the price ceiling
lowers surplus, it benefits consumers who do buy heating oil by
keeping the price down; in this way, it transfers surplus from sellers of heating oil to buyers. We'll explore a little later the idea of
using surplus-lowering policy to affect distributional goals.)

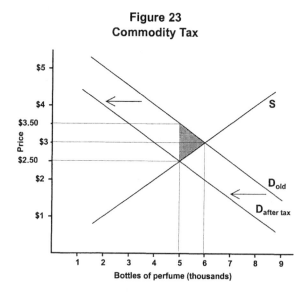

Figure 23
Commodity Tax

2. Commodity taxes. The effect of a $1.00 a bottle tax on perfume is represented by the shaded area in Figure 23 (a slightly modified version of Figure 14). Here, surplus drops relative to the maximum surplus that could be attained in a competitive market, and the forgone surplus is equal to the shaded area. The reason is similar to the one given above for the effect of a price ceiling. Namely, because of the tax, perfume that would cost less to make than the value placed on it isn't supplied, so surplus that could have been enjoyed isn't available to be enjoyed. For the 1,000 bottles of perfume not produced because of the tax, the cost of production would be less than the value placed on them. The bottles just over the 5,000th would cost about $2.50 each to produce and would be worth about $3.50 each to consumers, but they won't be produced, because their after-tax price would be $3.50 a bottle. Hence, people are basing their purchase decisions, not on the true, lower cost of production — $2.50 — but on the higher, tax-included figure. The surplus triangle representing the loss attributable to taxation is the *deadweight loss due to taxation.*

3. Imperfect Consumer Information

It is a commonplace that consumer information is often imperfect: we can't judge the quality of many goods and services on the basis of their outward appearance.

A. Importance

How important is the problem of imperfect information? It depends. For someone buying a hammer or an apple, the informational problem would probably not be great. We all pretty much know what hammers are used for and how apples taste, and our ability to make a judgment about a particular hammer or a particular apple, while not perfect, is not bad. We can tell a lot by looking at it. For someone buying newly created computer software, on the other hand, not very much may be known about its utility. The information that a person has also depends on the type of consumer that the individual is. For example, a repeat customer or a business customer who buys in large quantities would be likely to know a lot more than a one-time purchaser of a modest quantity would. Notable sources that consumers can turn to for information are advertising, reputation, and publications like *Consumer Reports*. In all, the significance of imperfect information is a function of context.

B. Problems: Inappropriate Purchases and Distorted Product Quality

Consumers make purchases on the basis of price and perceived characteristics of products and services. Thus, if the information they have is imperfect, they may make errors in their purchase decisions.

On one hand, consumers may mistakenly buy a good because they overestimate its value. A family may buy bottled water, for instance, in the belief that it's more healthful than tap water, whereas their tap water may actually be much cleaner than they think. Or a person may decide to go to see a particular movie because it has received good reviews, only to discover that it has been greatly overrated. When people mistakenly buy goods, there may be a loss in surplus, because the value they obtain may be less than the production cost.

On the other hand, consumers may mistakenly refrain from purchasing a good or service because they underestimate its true value. For example, I may not buy eggs because I think that the cholesterol in them will do me grave harm, yet the truth may be quite different. Here, surplus would be lost, because I don't eat eggs even though I really like them and would, if I knew the truth about them, value them more highly than their cost.

Another problem caused by lack of consumer information is that the quality of products supplied by firms may be distorted. Suppose that an automobile manufacturer knows that reinforced doors would significantly reduce injury in accidents, and suppose also that these doors would add an extra $100.00 to the price of the cars. Perhaps consumers would gladly pay the additional $100.00 if they understood the value of the doors. But if consumers lack this information and think that the doors have little value, they won't be willing to pay the $100.00. In this case, the car maker will not opt for the stronger doors: if it does, it will lose profits, because it can't charge the additional amount for the reinforced doors. Thus, as a result of consumer misperception, the quality of the product — the cars — will be lower than need be. The opposite side of the coin is that consumer misperception can lead to the addition of product features that lack any real intrinsic value. If consumers erroneously believe that the new features have a value that warrants the additional cost, these features will be incorporated into the product.

C. Policy Responses

There are several basic ways in which government can alleviate problems arising from imperfect consumer information.

1. Provide consumers with information. By providing consumers with information, government enables them to base their purchase decisions on correct information and thereby to avoid mistakes. For instance, consumers will not erroneously buy bottled water if they have been informed that it is no better than tap water. In addition, when government provides information to consumers, producers will produce goods of the quality that consumers really want, because consumers will recognize the true value of product characteristics and pay for good ones and not pay for bad ones. For example, a car maker will install reinforced doors if government crash tests show that such doors improve vehicle safety and government conveys this information about the value of reinforced doors to consumers.

Government can provide information to consumers, not only directly, but also indirectly, through grading and licensing of goods and services. When we see that milk is grade A or that a physician has graduated from a good medical school, we know that the milk or the physician meets certain quality standards.

Despite the importance of direct and indirect government provision of information to consumers, this mechanism for solving problems stemming from imperfect consumer information is not free from problems. First, the government must ascertain the quality of products and services. This isn't an easy task, especially in light of the complexity and changing nature of so many of our products and services. Second, transmitting information to consumers isn't necessarily cheap. As an example, television advertising about the risks of cigarette smoking isn't free. Third, the ability of consumers to absorb and understand information is limited. We are assaulted by all kinds of information in our daily lives and can't take anywhere near all of it into account. Thus, provision of information by government is a costly and imperfect process that inevitably leaves us somewhat ignorant about many products and services.

2. Regulate purchases. Another way in which government can attempt to solve problems associated with imperfect consumer information is by regulating purchases. On one hand, government can discourage the purchase of goods or services that it believes would not be in consumers' interests. One way that government can do this is simply by banning purchases — for example, by making it illegal for minors to buy cigarettes, on the premise that minors don't properly evaluate the hazards of smoking, or forbidding the sale of certain drugs over the counter, on the theory that the general population doesn't fully appreciate their usefulness and dangers. Government can prohibit individuals from providing a service unless they are licensed — for instance, it can prohibit nonphysicians from performing certain medical-care tasks. Yet another method is for government to impose taxes to discourage the purchase of goods, such as cigarettes.

In a similar vein, government can encourage the purchase of goods and services whose value consumers underestimate. It can do this by providing or subsidizing goods and services that are generally not fully appreciated. Although people who undervalue fire extinguishers might not ordinarily buy them, for example, they may do so if government subsidized the purchase.

What drawbacks are associated with regulation as a means of addressing the problems resulting from imperfect consumer information? And how does regulation compare with government provision of information? For one thing, administrative expense goes hand in hand with regulation of purchases, and it's hard to determine a priori how this expense compares to the cost of providing information. Another important factor is that regulation of purchases can be effective only if government has accurate information about consumer desires. For example, government may incorrectly believe that consumers want reinforced car doors. But perhaps people don't like the weight of the doors and their clunkiness, and perhaps they feel that money is better spent on side airbags as a way of improving safety in side-impact collisions. If so, and if government subsidized reinforced car doors, it would be erring. Or government may incorrectly believe that consumers would be harmed if they are allowed to decide for themselves whether to take a particular drug. If so, and if government makes the drug a prescription drug, it would be erring. In contrast, when government provides information about products to consumers, individuals can decide on the basis of their desires after considering the information whether to purchase those products. Hence, purchase decisions tend to be socially desirable.

3. Regulate product quality. Government can regulate product quality to address directly the problem of producers supplying inadequate quality because consumers lack information. In the case of car doors that manufacturers wouldn't strengthen even though doing so would be worth the $100.00 additional cost, government could mandate that cars have reinforced doors.

In comparing regulation of product quality with provision of consumer information as a remedy, the points that can be made are similar to those just made about regulation of purchases. Notably, the effectiveness of regulation of product quality depends on the quality of information government has about consumer desires. Providing information, if successful, would generally lead to better results.

4. Do nothing. The possibility that the best course is to do nothing should not be overlooked. Given the cost of providing information and the expense of and possible consumer harm from regulation, sometimes it's best for government to do nothing, especially when government information about consumer desires is only tolerably good.

Box 4
Should the Practice of Medicine
Be Limited to Doctors?

It has been proposed by well-known economists that any person be able to practice medicine. The role of the government would be mainly to *certify* how much medical education a person has, but the government would not require that a person have this or that amount of medical education to do what we now call practicing medicine. The main arguments in favor of this policy are that there are many medical care tasks that could be carried out fairly well by nonphysicians at far lower cost than now, when the tasks can only be performed by physicians. Hence, among other things, many people who now don't get medical care due to its high cost would get medical care, because it would be cheaper. The drawbacks to the policy include a concern that people would get inferior care from nonphysicians when they have serious illness. How do you react to this criticism, given the ability of government not only to certify medical practitioners, but also to advise people on which practitioners are capable of giving which kind of medical care?

4. Monopoly and Related Market Behavior

A monopoly is a market in which there is a single seller of a good or service. For instance, there may be just one movie theater in a small town. Some markets, though not monopolies, are far from perfectly competitive. These are markets where there is more than a single seller but not enough sellers to approximate perfect competition. An example is the market for burgers at fast-food chains like McDonald's, Burger King, and Wendy's.

A. Why Monopoly Arises

Monopoly arises in several ways. A single owner may purchase a crucial input to production, thereby preventing other firms from competing with it. This is nearly the case with De Beers, which owns a substantial fraction of the world's diamond-mining capacity.

Monopoly may also arise when a party has invented a new product and is given patent protection or has authored a work and is given copyright protection. The inventor enjoys a monopoly because the government has forbidden other companies to sell the product. Thus, the inventor of a drug, such as Viagra, will be a monopolist in that drug during the life of the patent.

In some circumstances, it is substantially cheaper for just one company to produce a good in large quantity than for many companies to produce it in smaller quantities. The result is what is referred to as a *natural monopoly*. This is the case, for example, with natural gas, which is cheaper to supply through a single network of gas lines owned by one company than through multiple networks owned by different companies. With just one network, the cost of the network can be spread over all the buyers of gas. If cost is significantly lower when a single company sells, that company is often able to maintain a monopoly position. A competitor's cost per customer would probably be high. Thus, competing with the established monopoly would be difficult, and the competitor's profit would likely not be sufficient to cover the cost of building another network. Moreover, in such natural monopoly situations, the government may grant an exclusive right to a single company to operate.

B. How a Monopolist Sets Price

The price that a monopolist sets is the one that maximizes its profits. To determine what this price is, the monopolist has to know how both its costs and its revenues change as its level of production changes. The goal is to adjust production to the level at which profits are at their maximum. The information that the monopolist needs can be derived from a variety of graphs. The best way for us to understand these graphs, or curves, is by working through them one by one.

The *total cost curve* is a graph of total production costs as a function of quantity produced (see Figure 24). Obviously, total costs go up as quantity produced increases.

The *marginal cost curve* shows how much more it costs to produce one additional unit. For the good represented in Figure 25, we can see that the marginal cost at a quantity of 120 is $5.00, meaning that to produce the 120th unit costs $5.00 more than it

Figure 24
Total Cost Curve

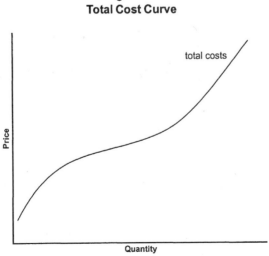

costs to produce the first 119 units. The marginal cost curve is often U-shaped, as it is in Figure 25. This is the case when the first units are expensive to produce because efficient techniques (e.g., involving division of labor, machines and equipment for mass production, and so forth) can't be employed. As more units are produced, however, the use of efficient techniques becomes feasible, and marginal cost declines. But at some point, marginal cost often begins to rise again, perhaps because capacity constraints necessitate the use of additional plant and equipment or because the company has to pay overtime or hire and train less-experienced employees.

The marginal cost curve is sometimes a flat line, when the added cost of producing each additional unit is the same, because capacity constraints and so forth are not relevant. For example, the marginal cost of producing a product like chairs might be constant because the cost of materials and labor used to make chairs remains essentially the same over a wide range of production levels.

Another curve of interest is the *average cost curve*. As the name implies, it's the graph of the average per-unit cost as a function of number of units produced. The average cost curve is often U-shaped, as the marginal cost curve is, and for similar reasons.

Figure 25
Marginal and Average Cost Curves

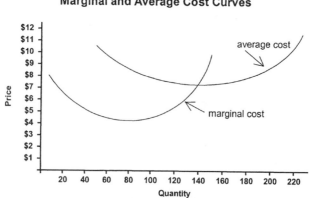

Average cost is high if a small number of units are produced, because various fixed costs are incurred (e.g., a plant has to be built or leased, basic machinery for production has to be purchased) regardless of the number of units produced. Then, as fixed costs are spread over a larger number of units and efficient production techniques become feasible, average cost falls. But ultimately, average cost rises again when capacity constraints are encountered.

Now let's turn our focus from the monopolist's costs to its revenue and ask how its revenue changes when it increases production. The change in revenue when one more unit is sold — that is, the amount of extra revenue obtained from the sale of an additional unit — is the *marginal revenue*. Consider the demand curve in Figure 26. If the monopolist is going to sell 20 units, it can charge $5.00 for each unit, and it will charge that amount. (If it charges more than $5.00, it will sell fewer than 20 units; if it charges less, it will receive less than it could have, and it wouldn't want to do this.) Therefore, the revenue will be $100.00 (i.e., 20 × $5.00 = $100.00). Now suppose that the monopolist decides to sell one more unit. Would its revenue increase by $5.00, the per-unit price it would charge if it were selling 20 units? The answer is no:

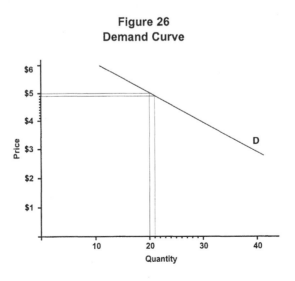

Figure 26
Demand Curve

in order to sell 21 units, the monopolist would have to lower the price slightly so as to induce the purchase of one more unit. It's evident from the demand curve that, to sell 21 units, the price must be lowered to $4.90 (see Figure 26). Therefore, the revenue from selling 21 units would be $102.90, whereas the revenue from selling 20 units is $100. The difference of $2.90 is the marginal revenue from selling the 21st unit. Note that the marginal revenue of $2.90 would be less than the $5.00 per-unit price at which 20 units could have been sold and also less than the $4.90 price at which the 21st unit would be sold. The reason is that the per-unit price would have been lowered by $.10 to induce the purchase of the 21st unit, so each of the 20 units that could have been sold at $5.00 (if only 20 units were going to be sold) would be sold for $.10 less. (More exactly, marginal revenue would be the $4.90 obtained from the 21st unit minus the $.10 decrease on each of the first 20 units — that is, minus $2.00 — which is $2.90.) Because, then, marginal revenue is generally less than price, the graph of marginal revenue is drawn below the demand curve, as in Figure 27.

Figure 27
Demand and Marginal Revenue Curves

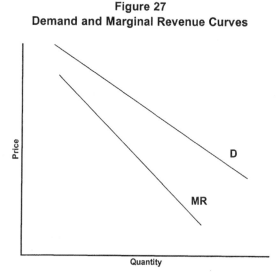

Figure 28
Demand Curve and Cost Curves

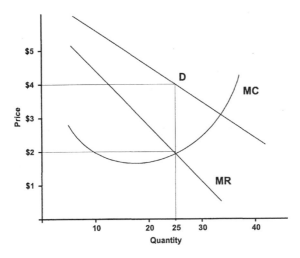

If the marginal cost curve and the demand and marginal revenue curves are put together on the same graph, the quantity that would maximize the monopolist's profits can be determined (see Figure 28).[6] It can be helpful to think of the process that the monopolist goes through in making this determination as a sequence of choices: produce the first unit if the revenue from selling it would exceed the cost of producing it; go on to produce the second unit if the marginal revenue it would yield exceeds the marginal cost of producing it; then produce the third unit if the marginal revenue would be greater than the marginal cost; and so on. Increasing production as long as marginal revenue exceeds marginal cost would make sense; doing so would enhance profit.

---

6. Alternatively, we could determine the *price* that would yield the greatest profit for the monopolist. However, the quantity approach turns out to be more helpful. (Of course, if we know the quantity that would maximize the monopolist's profit, in effect we know the price that would do the same: we can tell from the demand curve the price that can be charged for this quantity.)

In fact, profit is greatest at the level of production where marginal revenue exactly equals marginal cost. In Figure 28, marginal revenue matches marginal cost — $2.00 — at a quantity of 25. Hence, a quantity of 25 would yield maximum profit for the monopolist, and the price would be $4.00 per unit. Note that, were the monopolist to produce more than 25 units, marginal cost would exceed marginal revenue, and the profit would be less.

A point worth noting about the profit-maximizing behavior of the monopolist: the price it charges exceeds the marginal cost, as can be seen in Figure 28. That this is generally so follows from the geometry of the curves: the monopolist would produce the quantity at which marginal cost equals marginal revenue, and the marginal revenue curve must lie underneath the demand curve. This shouldn't come as a surprise. After all, charging a price that is higher than the marginal cost would be profitable.[7]

Optional material

> We can graphically describe the profit that the monopolist makes by adding to Figure 28 the average cost curve, as shown in Figure 29. The monopolist's profit is represented by the shaded area. The reason for this is that the average profit per unit is the price minus the average cost, which corresponds to the height of the shaded rectangle. If the average profit per unit is multiplied by the number of units sold, the result is total profit, which corresponds to the area of the shaded rectangle.

C. The Principal Economic Arguments Against Monopoly

The main disadvantage of monopoly, according to the classic economic argument, is that *the quantity sold is too low,* where "too low" means that *surplus would increase if the monopolist sold more units.* Look again at Figure 28 and recall that the monopolist maxi-

---

7. A closely related explanation emerges if we consider the quantity where marginal cost equals price — that is, where the marginal cost curve intersects the demand curve. Can you see why raising price would always enhance profit for the monopolist, meaning that price must exceed marginal cost?

Figure 29
Demand Curve, Cost Curves, and Monopoly Profit

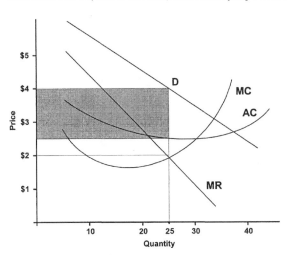

mizes profit when the price is $4.00 and the marginal cost is $2.00, which is lower than the price. The implication is that surplus would go up if another unit were produced: the value placed on this unit by the buyer would be approximately $4.00 and the marginal cost of production about $2.00, so $2.00 of additional surplus would be created. The reason the unit is *not* produced, of course, is that the monopolist has set the price at $4.00, which discourages another person from purchasing the good.

This forgone surplus can be represented graphically. In Figure 30, the shaded area corresponds to the unrealized surplus from all the units that the monopolist doesn't produce but for which marginal cost curve would be below the demand curve. This shaded triangle of forgone surplus is called the *deadweight loss due to monopoly*.

To understand the reality of the deadweight loss due to monopoly, think of a monopoly price and the implication of the price exceeding marginal cost. For example, a cable TV company charges $30.00 a month for service, but its marginal cost of service per

Figure 30
Deadweight Loss Due to Monopoly

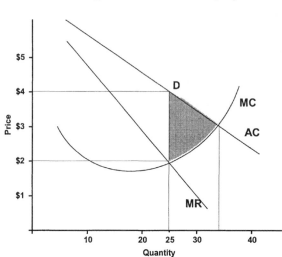

household is much less — say, $5.00. Any person who values service between $5.00 and $30.00 will not purchase it, so the surplus that could be derived from that person is forgone. Someone who values service at $20.00 a month will not purchase it, and $15.00 of surplus will be forgone as a result. There may be many such people, in which case the deadweight loss would be large.

The potential profit that a monopolist can earn might motivate a firm to spend significantly, but socially wastefully, to secure a monopoly position. This, too, is a social cost of monopoly. For example, a cable TV company might spend on lobbying to obtain an exclusive license to provide cable service in a city. The name given to efforts that a company makes to obtain or to maintain a monopoly position is *rent-seeking behavior,* for the company is seeking to capture the "rents" — that is, the profits — from being a monopolist. Rent-seeking expenditures are often unproductive and, to this extent, constitute a social cost associated with monopoly. Lobbying, for example, is not of direct value to consumers.

The monopolist makes a profit at the expense of buyers, and this is often viewed as a social cost, at least by the public at large. In other words, monopoly results in a distributional effect that favors the monopolist and harms consumers. We will discuss distributional issues a bit later, but for the present, it's sufficient to keep in mind that distributional effects don't influence surplus, as surplus is an aggregate number and is not altered by who enjoys it.

D. Price Discrimination

Although we assumed in the last section that the monopolist charges a single price for its product, in some circumstances a monopolist is able to, and wants to, charge different prices to different types of buyers — in other words, to engage in *price discrimination*. Some typical examples: airline travelers who book in advance are charged less than those who do not; children and the elderly are charged less than others for some goods and services; residential customers are charged less than businesses for telephone service; students are charged less for computers and software under educational discount programs than nonstudents who have to pay through typical retail channels.

1. Why and how price discrimination occurs. Monopolists engage in price discrimination because doing so allows them to match the prices they charge to the demand curve for particular groups of customers and thereby to enhance their profits. For example, children generally have a lower willingness to pay for movie tickets than adults do, so a movie theater may reap higher profits if it charges children less than adults, such as $4.00 rather than $8.00. If the theater must charge a single price, its profit won't be as great. By keeping the price high, at $8.00, for all individuals, it would lose many of its young customers, and thus its profits would fall, yet if it lowered the price to $4.00 for all customers, it would sacrifice substantial profits from its adult customers willing to pay $8.00.

To engage in price discrimination, a monopolist has to be able to do two things. First, it has to be able to distinguish different customers according to their willingness to pay. This is sometimes relatively easy, as in the case of a movie theater determining who is a child and who is not. Second, the monopolist must be able to prevent consumers from circumventing high prices. In the case of movie tickets, the theater has to be able to prevent adults from having children buy tickets for them. This, however, is probably not a serious problem. In the case of educational discounts on computers, the monopolist has to be able to prevent students from reselling purchased equipment to nonstudents; this can be difficult.

2. Is price discrimination socially undesirable? Price discrimination may be socially *desirable,* according to the surplus criterion, because it may increase the amount sold from the too-low level under monopoly with a single price. Equivalently, price discrimination may reduce the forgone surplus by allowing a monopolist both to charge high prices to those who are willing to pay a lot and to charge low prices to those who aren't willing to pay a lot, whereas the latter individuals would be unwilling to pay the high price if that were the only price the monopolist charged. For example, a movie theater fills more seats by allowing children to purchase tickets at a reduced price, like $4.00. If it charged the single price of $8.00, fewer children would buy tickets, and the empty seats would represent forgone surplus.

Price discrimination may also be socially desirable because the extra profit it generates may be what allows the monopolist to operate. Perhaps a movie theater would close if it weren't able to make the additional profit by selling children tickets for $4.00.

However, price discrimination is not necessarily socially desirable. One reason is that price discrimination might not increase sales. For example, it's possible that the prices a monopolist would charge to two subgroups of customers would result in lower total sales than a single price would. Another reason why price discrimination may not be socially desirable is that the effort expended to price discriminate — such as the effort that it takes for airlines to separate advance purchasers from others — is costly but not directly beneficial to consumers. Finally, the distributional effect of price discrimination (the higher profits that it results in for monopolists) is sometimes considered socially undesirable. However, as noted earlier, this is not a factor that affects its evaluation according to the surplus criterion.

E. Government Policy and Monopoly

The best type of government policy response to monopoly depends on the context and, notably, on the reasons for the monopoly's existence.

1. Monopoly and antitrust law. In the case of a monopoly that exists because the company has somehow established a monopoly position for itself and erected barriers to entry, the social costs of monopoly — the deadweight losses due to high prices and inadequate sales, and possibly the waste due to rent-seeking behavior — justify government intervention, at least in principle. Antitrust law would be an appropriate way to deal with this type of situation. In general, it addresses the problem of monopoly by *preventing the formation or continued existence of monopoly*. For example, if one company tried to buy all the movie theaters in the United States, antitrust law could prevent it from doing so. Or if the main burger chains — McDonald's, Burger King, and so forth — attempted to merge, the merger might not be allowed on the ground that it would create a monopoly. Additionally, antitrust law allows government to divide companies considered to be monopolies, as happened in 1911, when Standard Oil was broken up. However, antitrust law does not enable the government to force a monopoly to lower its price. A possible justification for this is that the government would face a huge difficulty in obtaining the information required to determine the correct price. [8]

2. Monopoly and intellectual property. In the case of a monopoly that exists because of a patent or copyright granted by the government, the policy response is quite different. It's true, of

---

8. However, as we'll see in a moment, in our discussion of natural monopoly, government does sometimes control the price that a monopoly charges.

course, that monopolies in patented drugs and copyrighted computer software and books cause deadweight losses. However, monopolies of these types are thought to have redeeming social benefits: they induce innovation and authorship. Indeed, the main purpose of the patent and copyright systems is to spur innovation and authorship by rewarding creators with monopoly profits. Society has made a judgment, in other words, that the social benefits of new creations engendered by the intellectual property rights system are worth the social cost of monopoly during the life of patents and copyrights. Hence, this kind of monopoly is not one that society wants to undermine. This is not to say that government shouldn't oversee particular aspects of the behavior of patent and copyright holders. For example, it should ensure that pharmaceutical firms holding patents on drugs don't obtain larger, broader protection than the law sets out. But it is to say that these monopolies are ones that we want to exist.

3. Natural monopoly and regulation. Another type of monopoly that society shouldn't seek to eliminate is the natural monopoly, such as one consisting of ownership of a network of gas lines. Doing so would mean losing cost savings, like those associated with having a single network of gas lines. However, it *would* be desirable to prevent the monopolist from charging the high monopoly price that it would want to charge, a price that would result in too little being sold and thus in deadweight losses. So, in the context of natural monopoly, there is a justifiable reason to subject the monopolist to *price regulation*.

What is the best form of price regulation? In the ideal, the allowed price should equal the marginal cost of production. Let's say that the marginal cost of gas is $.25 per unit. Anyone who values a unit of gas at more than $.25 would buy it, and this would lead to maximization of surplus. But in practice there are several problems with this kind of pricing scheme.

One shortcoming of marginal cost pricing is that, even though the revenue received would cover the gas company's marginal cost of production (i.e., the cost of securing the gas and maintaining the network), it wouldn't be sufficient to cover the high cost of constructing the network. Thus, to stay in business, the monopolist would need extra funds.

The problem of insufficient funds under marginal cost pricing can be solved in several ways. The government could give the gas company a subsidy. Alternatively, the price could be allowed to be higher than marginal cost, sufficiently high to cover the cost of network construction. In other words, the gas company could be allowed to charge a price equal to average cost. This approach, however, partially defeats the purpose of price regulation. If average cost is much higher than marginal cost — say, $1.00 per unit of gas — some people would be discouraged from making purchases even if the value they placed on a unit exceeded the marginal cost of $.25. (However, the monopoly price that an unregulated monopolist gas company would charge might be a lot higher than $1.00 per unit.)

Several other problems inherent in all regulated pricing schemes deserve mention. One is the difficulty that government regulators face in obtaining accurate information from the regulated monopolist. The monopolist has an incentive to skew what it reports to the regulator: it would be allowed to charge a higher price if it exaggerated its costs. A second problem is that the monopolist has little motive to hold costs down if the price it's allowed to charge is based on these costs. A third problem is that regulators may be "captured" by industry — for example, regulators may leave government service and work for industry — and end up serving industry's interests rather than the public's.

An alternative to regulation would be for government itself to own and operate the monopoly, such as the network of gas lines. Gas could then be priced at marginal cost. But some people question government's ability to operate business efficiently because of various constraints it faces.

F. Oligopoly and Monopolistic Competition

As mentioned earlier, sometimes there is more than one seller but
not so many that the situation would be described as highly competitive. Situations of this type are often referred to generically
as ones of *imperfect competition*. The sellers may be offering identical products — such as gas stations that sell the same type of
gasoline — or fairly closely related products, such as the burgers
sold by McDonald's and Burger King. Imperfect competition is
complicated to describe because of the number of types of inter-
actions that may exist among a small number of sellers, who are
aware of each other's existence and who compete strategically.

To understand the range of possibilities and some of the issues,
let's consider the example of two gas stations, Bill's and Sue's,
located near each other and selling essentially identical gasoline.
Let's assume that the two stations have to sell at the same price
— otherwise, customers would flock to the cheaper station. If the
cost of a gallon of gasoline for each station is $1.00, what price
would we expect the stations to charge consumers?

One possibility is that the price would be driven by competition between the two stations down to $1.00, with neither station
making a profit. At a higher price, say $1.20, one station, say Bill's,
would cut its price to $1.19 in order to steal all customers from
Sue's. So, if Bill and Sue had been dividing the market when the
price was $1.20 and making a $.20 profit on each gallon, Bill would
now make a profit of $.19 per gallon from the *entire* market and
thus do much better. (It's much more profitable to sell 200 gallons and get a $.19 profit per gallon than to sell 100 gallons and
get a $.20 profit per gallon.) Sue, however, would immediately
notice Bill's price reduction and the disappearance of her customers, and she would lower her price. She might match Bill's
price of $1.19, so they would again share the market, but in this
case each would make only a $.19 profit per gallon. Alternatively,
Sue might undercut Bill and charge $1.18, stealing the entire mar-
ket from him but making only $.18 per gallon. In either case, Bill

might retaliate, and the process might go on until each is charging $1.00, at which point neither would undercut the other, for doing so would only result in losses.

Because lowering the price to $1.00, equal to cost, would lead to the elimination of their profits, it might seem unlikely that they would go this route. We might expect them to realize or to have learned from experience that price wars spell ruin in the end. An attractive approach would be for Bill and Sue to make an explicit agreement — that is, collude — to set a high price. By acting as a unit, they could set the single monopoly price, perhaps $1.20 or more, that maximizes their joint profits. Thus, they have an incentive to collude. However, collusive agreements about price violate the antitrust laws and are penalized. If Bill and Sue conspire to set price and are found out, they will suffer sanctions. An additional possibility is that Bill and Sue might come to a tacit accommodation not to undercut each other.

The issues that we have been looking at arise in many settings, and traditionally they are ascribed mainly to oligopoly. *Oligopoly* usually refers to markets in which the number of firms is between two and some not very large number, say 10, and in which these firms consciously take into account how the other firms will react to what they do as well as how the firms might collude.

The term *monopolistic competition* applies to markets where the number of firms is larger than in oligopoly (say, all the barbershops in a city), where each firm has a somewhat different product from the others (each barbershop has a unique location and perhaps a unique style of hair-cutting), and where the firms don't really take into account how the others will react to what they do individually. A point about monopolistic competition that is emphasized concerns entry into the industry: firms join the market until supernormal profits are competed away. Thus, although each firm is a mini-monopolist in a sense, it doesn't make substantial profits, because entry lowers its demand curve (e.g., barbershops enter into business in the city until most of them aren't making very large profits, even though each has a somewhat unique product).

5. Externalities

A. What Are Externalities?

One party's action is said to create an *externality* if it influences the well-being of another person. To give you an idea of the generality of externalities, consider the following examples:

- *Nuisance.* When a person disturbs his neighbors by making noise, producing foul odors, allowing a misbehaving pet to roam free, and the like, he is commonly said to be creating a nuisance.

- *Pollution.* When a firm discharges an undesirable substance into a body of water or into the air, it reduces the utility of others who use the water or breathe the air.

- *Dangerous, risk-creating behavior.* When somebody speeds on the road, he or she is creating the risk of an accident; when a construction firm fails to take the precaution of fencing off its work site, it's creating the risk of an accident if children wander by.

- *Use of a common resource.* One person's use of a resource, such as a beach or a pasture, may harm others: the user of the beach may litter, the user of the pasture may overgraze his animals, causing erosion of the pastureland.

- *Salutary behavior.* A person's actions may occasionally help not only him but others as well, as where an apiarist's bees help to pollinate a nearby farmer's fruit trees, or where a person beautifies his land, to the advantage of others who will see it as well.

- *Behavior that has a psychological effect on others.* My actions may have ramifications for others even though there is no physical effect on them; the influence may be purely psychological. The very fact that others know that I am praying to a strange God may affect them and thus may constitute an externality.

As these examples show, externalities are many and varied in nature, they may be beneficial for, or detrimental to, the affected party, may have effects contemporaneously or in the future, and may be probabilistic in character.

B. The Problem of Externalities: Private Behavior Is Not Socially Desirable

A socially desirable act, given the social goal of maximizing surplus, is one for which the benefits exceed the costs, where the benefits and costs should include all externalities. The problem that externalities create is that those who make decisions about acts with externalities do not naturally take into account the external effects — because they are not experienced by the decision makers. Hence, decisions will tend to be inappropriate, and in two possible ways.

The first problem is that there will be too much activity that causes external harms. For example, a factory might burn waste and derive a $1,000 benefit from this (because it does not have to haul the wastes to a dump), even though the cost to neighbors who dislike smoke is $5,000. In general, we would expect nuisances, pollution, dangerous behavior, and the whole range of actions that create detrimental externalities to be observed more often than is socially desirable, unless something happens to correct the problem.

The second problem created by externalities is the converse of what we just mentioned, namely, that there will be too little activity that generates external benefits. A person might decide not to landscape his or her yard at a cost of $1,000 because the value he or she personally would derive is only $500, whereas those living in the neighborhood would together place a value of $900 on the landscaping, so the total value of $1,400 would make land-scaping socially desirable.

C. Resolution of Externality Problems Through Bargaining

Externality problems can sometimes be resolved through bargaining. However, obstacles can get in the way of bargaining.

1. Frictionless bargaining and the desirable resolution of externality problems. Suppose that bargaining between the creator of an externality and the parties affected by it is frictionless: bargaining will take place, and a mutually beneficial agreement about externalities will be concluded whenever such an agreement exists in principle. This means that any externality problem that is desirable to eliminate will be eliminated — because any undesirable action will be forestalled by bargaining and agreement. In the example of the burning of waste by the factory, an agreement in which the neighbors who would suffer harm of $5,000 pay an amount between $1,000 and $5,000 — say $3,000 — for waste not to be burned will be mutually desirable. For receiving $3,000 and not burning waste is preferable to the factory to burning waste, which saves it only $1,000; and paying $3,000 is preferable to the neighbors to suffering harm of $5,000.[9] In the example of the landscaping that ought to be carried out, the neighbors will be willing to pay an amount between $500 and $900, such as $700, for the person to undertake the landscaping. If he is paid $700, then after paying $1,000 for the landscaping, he will enjoy a benefit of $500, so his net benefit is $200 and he will be

---

9. Note as well that if the neighbors have the right to prevent smoke, the factory would not be willing to pay enough to secure permission to generate smoke, for that would require at least $5,000. Hence, the outcome would be the same. This point, that the allocation of legal rights does not affect the outcome when there is bargaining, and that the outcome maximizes surplus, is known as the Coase Theorem. It was emphasized in an influential article by Ronald Coase (The Problem of Social Cost, *Journal of Law and Economics*, 1960, vol. 3, 1–44).

better off than if he had not landscaped; also, the neighbors will have paid $700 for a $900 benefit, so they too will be better off.

2. Asymmetric information may stymie bargaining. We have been assuming that when mutually beneficial agreements exist, such agreements will be made. But experience tells us that success in making agreements is not guaranteed, and as economists emphasize generally, an explanation involves asymmetric information between parties that leads to miscalculations in bargaining. Suppose that the neighbors who would be disturbed by smoke think that the benefit to the factory of burning waste is probably only $100 (rather than the true $1,000), and they offer only $200 to induce the factory not to burn the waste. The factory would refuse this offer, and there might be an impasse in bargaining. Such misgauging of the other side's true situation can

---

Box 5
Reluctance to Bargain

Many people who are disturbed by someone else, such as by a noisy neighbor, are quite reluctant to discuss the matter with them, and it's not because of the time it would take. Rather, it's due to a psychological aversion to bargaining, to the unpleasantness of having to confront openly a person in a situation of conflicting interests. This can be a quite powerful "cost" that stands in the way of bargaining as a means of resolving externality problems. Another factor that often prevents bargaining as a resolution is that people are hesitant to make payments to resolve problems like noise. If you were to offer your neighbor $50 to have his noisy party end by midnight, this might make you seem mercenary and might somehow insult the neighbor (people are supposed to be considerate of each other because this is right, not because they are paid to behave that way).

easily lead to failures to agree, even though both sides are acting rationally given their information.

3. Bargaining may not even occur. Not only may bargaining not succeed, due to problems of asymmetric information. It may not even get off the ground, for any of several important reasons.

a. Distance between parties. If the potentially concerned parties aren't physically proximate, bargaining may be difficult to arrange. For example, a driver who is contemplating speeding in an automobile can hardly bargain with potential victims of accidents, for they aren't nearby (and are unknown) when the driver puts his foot to the gas pedal. Or a person who is at the point of deciding whether to erect a fence that the neighbor might regard as objectionable may find that the neighbor is on vacation at an unknown location, so can't be contacted about an alternative, possibly superior agreement (such as sharing the higher cost of planting a screen of trees instead of installing the fence).

b. Number of parties. If the number of involved parties is large, the likelihood that all can come together to bargain may be small, because of coordination difficulties, which tend to increase with the number of parties. In addition, the motivation to bargain may diminish as the number of parties increases. If, for example, each individual in a neighborhood believes that the others can be depended on to engage in bargaining for an agreement that will benefit the individual, such as for a factory to stop blowing its whistle early in the morning, then no one, or too few people, will participate in bargaining with the factory to obtain the agreement. This problem of free-riding on others' efforts may be acute if the benefits that would be gained from bargaining are individually small.

c. Lack of knowledge of external effects. Clearly, someone who isn't aware that a future loss or benefit is at stake is unlikely to engage in bargaining. If I live near a factory and don't know that I'm at risk of developing cancer from its discharges, then I will hardly bargain for a change in its behavior.

D. Resolution of Externality Problems Through Markets

Another way in which externality problems may be resolved is through the operation of certain markets. One example is market-able pollution rights, which are rights that firms may purchase that allow them to generate pollution. Because firms have to pay for the right to generate pollution, they will not pollute unless the benefit they derive from doing so exceeds the cost. Another example is the market for the pollination services of bees. Farmers who want to improve their fields purchase the services of bees (which are transported to their farms) in a well-organized market. From the perspective of the beekeepers, hiring out their bees provides an additional source of income. Thus, beekeepers will tend to raise bees when they should — that is, when the total benefits from the honey produced and the pollination services outweigh the cost of raising the bees. Such instances of externalities being resolved by organized markets are, however, unusual. (Can you explain why the problem of a factory whose smoke bothers just the immediate neighbors can't be resolved by an organized market?)

E. Resolution of Externality Problems Through Legal Rules

Just as some externality problems may be resolved through bargaining or markets, others may be addressed through legal rules of various types. We'll focus on just several of the important types.

1. Types of rule. Under direct *regulation*, the state directly constrains behavior to reduce externality problems. For example, a factory may be prevented from generating pollution that may present a health hazard; a fishing vessel may be required to limit its catch to help reverse depletion of a fishery; or a person may be prevented by a zoning ordinance from opening a business establishment in a residential area in order to preserve its ambience.

Closely related to regulation is assignment of property rights and their protection at the request of parties who hold the rights. Assuming that people have the right to clean air, for example, they can prevent a firm from polluting by asking the state to intervene. The complaining party obtains an *injunction* against the injurer, and the police powers of the state are then brought to bear to enforce the injunction.

Society can also make use of financial incentives to reduce harmful externalities. Under *tort liability*, parties who suffer harm can bring suit against injurers and obtain compensation for their losses. Having to pay for the harm they inflict will motivate injurers to reduce the amount of harm they cause.[10]

Another financial incentive to reduce harm is the corrective tax (sometimes called the *Pigouvian tax*, after the economist Pigou, who was the first to study externalities). Under it, a party makes a payment to the state equal to the harm the party is expected to cause — for example, a firm pays for the harm that discharge of a pollutant into a lake is likely to cause. The corrective tax is similar to tort liability in that it creates a financial incentive to reduce harm, for an injuring party will reduce harm in an effort to avoid having to pay a tax equal to expected harm. However, there are differences between the corrective tax and tort liability. A corrective tax reflects anticipated harm (the harm the pollution is expected to cause), whereas tort liability is liability for harm actually done. Another difference is that the corrective tax is paid to the state, whereas tort liability payments are made to victims.

2. Comparison of rules. Let's sketch the comparison of the foregoing legal rules for controlling externalities, focusing one at a time on a list of factors that are relevant to the operation of the rules.

a. Information of the state. If the state has complete information about acts, that is, knows the injurer's benefit and the victim's harm, then each of the rules leads to optimality. To amplify in terms of the example of pollution, suppose that the state can ascertain whether the cost of the smoke arrestor is less than the harm from pollution and thus determine whether it is best to prevent pollution. If that is so, the state can accomplish its purpose

---

10. The assumption here is that the injurer must pay for any harm caused and thus that the rule is strict liability. We do not consider the negligence rule, under which the injurer pays for harm caused only if the injurer was negligent.

by regulation: it can forbid pollution. The state can also achieve optimality by giving the property right to clean air to the victim. The state can also employ tort liability. This will lead the injurer not to cause harm because he would have to pay for it, and harm exceeds his benefit. Similarly, under the corrective tax he would not pollute.

If the state doesn't have complete information about harm and benefit, however, it can't determine with certainty whether or not an action like polluting should take place. Hence, the state can't necessarily achieve optimality through regulation or assignment of property rights, for to do so, it would have to know what action is optimal. For instance, under regulation, if the harm from pollution would be 100 and the state doesn't know whether the cost of an arrestor would be 75 or 150, it doesn't know whether or not to require installation of the arrestor.

Yet as long as the state has information about the magnitude of harm, it can achieve optimality under tort liability or the corrective tax. Under these approaches, the injurer compares the cost of installing the arrestor to liability or the tax for harm: the injurer will cause pollution if and only if the cost of the arrestor exceeds the harm, which is optimal. The virtue of tort liability and the corrective tax is that they harness the information that injurers have about the cost of reducing harm or the benefit they would obtain from acting, by making them compare the cost or benefit to the harm.

b. Information of victims. Information of victims is relevant to the functioning of the rules requiring victims to play a role in enforcement. Namely, for victims to bring injunctions to prevent harmful acts and protect their property rights, they have to know who might harm them, such as who might pollute, and what the harm would be if it occurred. If the pollution is colorless and odorless and inflicts harm only over time, they might be totally unaware of the pollution and its long-range effects and thus wouldn't have the knowledge they would need to bring an injunction. Similarly, for tort liability to function, victims must know both that harm occurred and who caused it. For regulation or corrective taxation to function, victims don't need such information. The state imposes corrective taxes or regulates regardless of whether victims know who is causing them harm or understand its nature.

c. Administrative costs. Administrative costs are the costs borne by the state and the parties in association with the use of a legal rule. Tort liability has a general administrative cost advantage over the other rules in that the legal system becomes involved only if harm is done, whereas under the other approaches, the legal system is involved whether or not harm occurs. This advantage may be significant, especially when the likelihood of harm is small. Nevertheless, administrative costs are sometimes low under the non-liability approaches. For example, determining whether a party is in compliance with regulation is easy in some circumstances (e.g., determining whether factory smokestacks are sufficiently high would be) and may be done through random monitoring, saving resources. Also, levying a corrective tax can be inexpensive if, for instance, it's paid at the time a product is purchased (e.g., a firm could be made to pay the tax when it buys the fuel that causes pollution). In the end, the particulars of the situation at hand have to be examined in order to determine which type of rule is superior on grounds of administrative cost.

d. Ameliorative behavior of victims. Victims can often take steps to reduce harm (e.g., they can purchase clothes dryers rather than hang laundry outdoors, where it can be soiled by smoke). This is a desirable approach when taking these steps is sufficiently cheap and effective (accounting, of course, for the injurer's opportunity to reduce harm). Under regulation, corrective taxation, and other approaches that don't compensate victims for the harm they experience, victims have a natural incentive to take optimal precautions because they bear their own losses. Under tort liability, however, this incentive would be lacking to the extent that victims will be compensated for the losses they suffer.

```
┌──────────────────────────────────────────┐
│                  Box 6                     │
│           If Taxes Are So Good,            │
│         Why Are They So Rarely Used?       │
│                                            │
│    Economists have traditionally favored   │
│  taxes as the best cure for harmful        │
│  externalities, like pollution. Yet        │
│  taxes are rarely used to prevent harmful  │
│  effects. The main tools that all          │
│  societies employ to combat harmful        │
│  effects are regulation and liability. To  │
│  understand why, think about the mundane   │
│  problem of people leaving their           │
│  sidewalks icy, which can lead to          │
│  accidents. How would a tax work to        │
│  correct this? Would it be based on        │
│  measurements of the amount of ice that is │
│  left on the sidewalks? On the foot        │
│  traffic on the sidewalks? Wouldn't this   │
│  be very expensive to administer? By       │
│  contrast, what would be the nature of     │
│  administrative costs under regulation?    │
│  Under liability for actual harm that      │
│  occurs due to icy sidewalks?              │
└──────────────────────────────────────────┘
```

e. Ability of injurers to pay. For tort liability to induce potential injurers to behave appropriately, they must have assets sufficient to make the required payments. Otherwise, they would have inadequate incentives to reduce harm. This is especially relevant in settings where the potential harm is sufficiently large to exceed the assets of the potential injurer (e.g., a fire could cause a harm that exceeds the assets of the owner of the property; an explosion at a factory or a leak of toxic material could cause much more harm than the company's assets are worth). Inability to pay is likely to be less of a problem for the corrective tax, which equals the expected harm, an amount generally less than the actual harm. In situations where inability to pay is a problem, regulation and the other approaches become more appealing.

f. Conclusion. This review of factors bearing on the effectiveness of the rules suggests that their relative strengths depend very much on the context. Let's consider the classic problem of pollution caused by the burning of fuel at factories. Liability might be expected not to work well because the victims might have difficulty ascertaining that they were harmed and determining who was responsible. The injunction might not function well for similar reasons. Regulating the amount of fuel burned would be unappealing, because doing so would require the state to determine the optimal amount, meaning that it would have to determine the value of production or the cost of alternative fuels, either of which would depend on many particulars that would be expensive, if not impractical, for the state to learn. Thus, the corrective tax, relying only on the state's knowledge of the harm that the pollution tends to cause, becomes appealing.

6. Public Goods

A. Definition

Goods (or services) that are nonexcludable and nonrival are called *public goods* by economists. Goods are *nonexcludable* if people can't be prevented from enjoying them. Two examples are national defense and fireworks displays: we can't be prevented from benefitting from national defense, and we can't be prevented from viewing a nearby fireworks display. Goods are *nonrival* if one person's use doesn't diminish another person's. This, too, is true of both national defense and fireworks displays: my benefitting from national defense doesn't reduce your benefitting from it, and my viewing of a fireworks display doesn't diminish your viewing of it. Other stock examples of public goods include lighthouses, city streets, radio programs, and basic research. (Can you say why each of these is nonexcludable and nonrival?) Let's note that sometimes one person's use of a public good will, in a limited way, detract from another person's use. This may be the result of congestion: if many people are at a fireworks display, the views of children and short people will be blocked; if many people are using the city streets, traffic will be impeded. For now, however, we'll set this matter aside.

B. Ideal Supply

In principle, society often wants public goods to be supplied. In terms of the surplus criterion, society wants a public good supplied if its value to the individuals who would enjoy it exceeds the cost of supplying it. Thus, a lighthouse ought to be built if its value to all the ships that would benefit from its beacon outweighs the cost of its construction and operation.

C. Inadequate Supply by the Private Sector

It is apparent that public goods will not be adequately supplied by the private sector. The reason is plain: because people can't be excluded from using public goods, they can't be charged money for using them, so a private supplier can't make money from providing them. For instance, no ship would pay for the services of a lighthouse, because it could benefit from the lighthouse even if it didn't pay. Hence, no entrepreneur would build a lighthouse. Likewise, no company could make money selling national defense to individuals, because all individuals would benefit from national defense even if they didn't pay for it. Thus, national defense wouldn't be privately supplied. Even though many public goods are eminently socially worthwhile, they will not be supplied by the private sector.

D. Public Provision

Because public goods are generally not adequately supplied by the private sector, they have to be supplied by the public sector.

Box 7
Lighthouses

Lighthouses have been very important to the safety of shipping, especially in antiquity. One of the greatest construction projects in ancient history was of the giant lighthouse Pharos in Alexandria, Egypt. Although economic theory predicts that lighthouses have to be built by the state, Ronald Coase wrote an article critical of economic theorizing, for he discovered that for over a century most lighthouses in Britain were built and operated by private individuals for profit! But how could the lighthouse owners have collected fees from ships? Later investigation revealed the answer: the state *forced* ships to pay lighthouses, for instance, by not letting ships leave port without making payment. So the lighthouses weren't really supplied in the usual way by the private sector after all, and the message of economic theory about lighthouses remains intact.

Thus, a lighthouse that is desirable to supply, because its benefits to all users outweigh its costs, can be built by the state. The same holds true for streets, national defense, basic research, and so forth. This is the basic argument for public supply of public goods (and the reason why they are referred to as public goods).

Several problems are associated with the public provision of public goods, however. One is the need for the government to obtain information about the benefits and costs of the goods, in order to determine whether they are worth supplying. A notable difficulty is that people have an incentive to distort the truth when questioned about the value they place on public goods. When asked whether they want a fireworks display (or a street extended), those who want this would have an incentive to report a very high number as their valuation: exaggerating the truth would cost them nothing. For this and other reasons, government faces a problem in deciding which public goods are worthwhile supplying. Other problems with public provision of public goods stem from the imperfections of the political process and the cost of raising funds through taxation for the purchase of public goods.

E. Qualifications

One qualification to the general argument that public goods have to be publicly provided is that, in some contexts, private parties can convert a public good into an excludable good and, being able to charge for it, might supply it. For instance, a company that wants to make money from a fireworks display could erect a tall fence around the display area and charge for entry; a company that wants to profit from constructing a road could erect and operate toll booths at all entrances to the road. Thus, some fireworks displays and some roads would be supplied by the private sector. However, note that the private supplier would be able to act as a monopolist and charge a monopoly price, causing deadweight losses. Moreover, private supply of public goods involves the expense of excluding nonpayers — the cost of fencing off the area around the fireworks display and the cost of constructing and staffing toll booths at entrances to the road. Such expenses need not be borne by the state under public provision, so the expenses constitute a disadvantage of private provision.

The other qualification concerns the possibility noted earlier, that a public good may not be entirely nonrival, principally because its use leads to congestion. Congestion effects (e.g., those resulting from too many people viewing a fireworks display or using a road) make it socially desirable to limit use of a public good to those who place a higher value on using it than they contribute to its congestion. If each person who uses a road imposes a cost of $5.00 on others in terms of congestion, only those individuals who value using the road at more than $5.00 should use it. Hence, it may be best for the road, if publicly provided, to be a toll road for which $5.00 is the toll.[11]

F. Direct Versus Indirect Public Provision

Although the private market would not be expected to supply various public goods, the public need not provide them directly. Rather than providing a good itself — for example, building roads, erecting a lighthouse, or conducting basic research — the government can pay a private company to provide it.

---

11. Whether it's best for a public provider of the road to charge for use depends on the cost of erecting toll booths and collecting tolls. If the congestion effect would be small, allowing congestion would be better than incurring the cost of charging tolls for use of the road.

7. Welfare Economics

A. What Is Welfare Economics?

The term *welfare economics* refers to the organizing framework that economists have for analyzing so-called *normative* questions, those of the form, What policy *should* we adopt? Questions of this type are to be distinguished from *descriptive* questions, which are of the form, What will the *effect* of a policy be? Descriptive questions are concerned with identifying the results of a policy, not with evaluating the social goodness or badness of the results. The task of *evaluation* is that of welfare economics.

B. Individual Well-Being

An important factor to consider in evaluating policies is, of course, the well-being of individuals. Economists use the notion of an individual's *utility* to refer to the person's well-being. The concept of utility is completely general and thus encompasses not only conventional elements of a person's happiness — the material comforts of life and the things that a person selfishly cares about — but also any aesthetic pleasures and any satisfaction derived from helping relatives, friends, and mankind in general or from doing one's duty in any sense that the individual conceives to be important. *Anything* that pleases a person is, by definition, something that augments that person's utility.

C. Social Welfare

Economists evaluate social well-being by referring to a measure of social welfare. This measure is typically built up from things that matter to individuals in some way.

For example, in this chapter we've been using surplus (aggregate benefits to people minus costs of production) as the measure of social welfare. We've said that market outcomes are socially desirable because they maximize this measure of social welfare, and we've said that monopoly is socially undesirable because it does not. We have focused on the surplus measure because it has two important properties that we presume most ways of measuring social welfare would have in common: (1) that when individuals' benefits rise and people become happier, social welfare rises, and (2) that when costs go up and people who bear the costs become less happy, social welfare falls.

Even though we've emphasized the surplus measure of social welfare, as is conventional, we've done so mainly because of its analytical convenience. In general, *economists do not assume that any specific measure of social welfare is objectively correct.* Different measures appeal to different people. Whatever measure is used, however, the objective for the person who endorses it is to maximize it. Measures of social welfare include the following:

- *Classical utilitarianism:* The utilities of individuals are added together and maximized.
- *Other functions of individuals' utilities:* Many measures of social welfare are different from utilitarianism yet depend on the utilities of individuals. For example, consider a function equal to the sum of utilities minus a "penalty" that depends on the variability of utilities in the population. This measure of social welfare depends on the distribution of utilities, because the more disparate the distribution is, the higher the penalty is, and thus the lower social welfare is. Another example is the so-called maximin criterion associated with the philosophical position of Rawls: social welfare is assumed to equal the utility of the least well off person in the population; hence, the social goal is to maximize the well-being of the least well off person (thus, the term *maximin*).

- *Factors other than individuals' utilities:* Many measures of social welfare depend on factors that are distinct from individuals' utilities. For instance, social welfare might be a function of individuals' utilities and, in addition, it might decline whenever some notion of fairness is violated (such as the notion that wrongdoers should be punished in proportion to the gravity of their bad acts), regardless of the effect of maintaining the notion of fairness on individuals' utilities.[12]

Box 8
Rawlsian "Maximin" Social Objective

According to the Rawlsian criterion, social welfare is taken to equal the utility of the least well off person, so the social objective is to maximize the utility of this least fortunate person – the entire focus is on this person. Thus, for example, suppose that there are 99 people in a hospital who can be greatly helped by getting medical attention but who won't die without it, and 1 virtually comatose person on the edge of death whose life can be prolonged slightly by getting lavish attention. Then to promote the Rawlsian criterion, *all* the medical resources would go to making the virtually comatose person live a bit longer, none would go to the 99 who would be made substantially better off by receiving medical attention.

---

12. Thus, even if punishment doesn't affect anyone's well-being by, for example, encouraging deterrence, incapacitation, or reform, it should be imposed in order to promote the notion of fair punishment and the measure of social welfare depending upon it.

Because *any* notion of the social good can be cast as a measure of social welfare, the social welfare framework, from the perspective of economists, is more a language or organizing tool for analysis than it is a system of thinking that embodies restrictions on what constitutes the social good. As an analytical aid, it has proved to be very powerful.

Economists typically restrict their attention to measures of social welfare that depend *solely* on individuals' utilities. They usually don't consider ones of the third type described above (i.e., ones depending on factors other than individuals' utilities). Such measures tend to lack appeal because, by hypothesis, they depend on something that *no* person cares about. In fact, it can be demonstrated that any measure of social welfare that depends, even in part, on a factor that no one cares about leads to the following possibility: policy A, which promotes the factor that no one cares about, may be ranked higher than policy B, even though *all* individuals prefer policy B. This fact — that any measure of social welfare that depends at all on an element that no one cares about leads in some situations to contravention of the unanimous preferences of individuals — makes such a measure of social welfare unappealing.

Although we'll assume that measures of social welfare depend solely on individuals' utilities, we're left with a very wide scope for consideration, from utilitarianism to any type that deems the distribution of well-being important. The economic view of desirable social choice is this: *given* a measure of social welfare, what social policy is best? The question of what measure of social welfare should be considered is often not part of the economist's inquiry, so the inquiry about social choice is of a conditional nature.

D. Social Welfare Maximum: Efficiency and Distribution

We can ask the hypothetical question, given the natural and human resources available to us, and our technology, what would truly maximize social welfare? Although the particular answer will depend on the measure of social welfare, we can usefully describe the answer as being composed of two steps: first produce goods and services in the most *efficient* manner, and then *distribute* them so as to maximize the measure of social welfare. Consider a simple world with just one produced good, pie, that everybody wants more of. Then what is socially optimal under any measure of social welfare is for the net amount of pie produced to be as large as possible — this is efficiency — and then for the pie to be sliced up and distributed in a way that is best according to the particular measure of social welfare under consideration. If the measure is highest when people have equal shares, then that is how the pie would be divided, for instance.

E. Social Welfare and the Market

There is a connection between the market and the hypothetical social welfare maximum just discussed. Suppose that society can costlessly redistribute wealth. Then the following is true: Regardless of the measure of social welfare, the social welfare maximum can be achieved by redistributing wealth and allowing competitive markets to function.[13] The idea behind this *central theorem* of welfare economics is that markets will lead to efficient production of goods and services, and that appropriately designed redistribution of wealth will accomplish the desired allocation of utilities among individuals. To maximize a measure of social welfare that favors equality, for instance, wealth would be redistributed so as to achieve equality.

F. Answers to Questions and Common Criticisms

A number of questions and criticisms are frequently raised about welfare economics.

1. How does the fact that redistribution is not costless — notably, that income taxation dilutes work effort — affect the statement just made about social welfare maximization and

---

13. This statement presumes that there are no problems of consumer information, no harmful externalities, or other factors impeding market functioning.

the market? It's generally thought that the income tax system dulls work incentives; certainly if one faced a 90 percent income tax rate, the incentive to work overtime, to work extra years before retirement, or to start a business rather than work for salary, would be reduced. Thus, the attempt to redistribute via the income tax system turns out to reduce the amount of income that there is redistribute. In other words, the act of slicing up the pie — the redistributive step represented by income taxation and transfers — shrinks the size of the pie.

The implications of this important point are several. First, the hypothetical social optimum of the central theorem of welfare economics cannot be achieved. Second, the practically achievable social welfare optimum in general involves a tradeoff between the reduction in output caused by redistribution — the so-called efficiency loss due to income taxation — and the benefits of redistribution in terms of raising social welfare. Thus, there will be less redistribution than in the ideal. How much less will depend on how much efficiency is lost as a result of the attempt to redistribute. If the social welfare function endorsed would, in the ideal, result in an equal distribution of income, the optimal distribution, given the effect of income taxation on work effort, might allow considerable inequality of income.

2. Should policy evaluation be influenced by distributional concerns, given the existence of an income tax and a transfer system that can be used to redistribute? Both efficiency and distributional factors are generally of importance to social welfare and thus would seem to matter in the evaluation of social policy. However, the existence of an income tax and transfer system that can be used to redistribute suggests that policies should be judged solely in terms of their efficiency effects. The kernel of the argument behind this claim is that, if a policy results in undesirable distributional effects, they can be remedied by the income tax (and transfer) system. For example, consider policies like price ceilings on drugs that are intended to benefit poor people but that may retard incentives of drug companies to develop new drugs. If society feels that drug prices have too great an impact on the poor, the problem can be remedied by adjusting the income tax system (e.g., by reducing taxes on the poor, by giving them credits for drug purchases, and the like). Compromising incentives to develop drugs in order to help the poor is socially unwise because they can be aided without diminishing incentives.[14]

3. Do economists believe that the market is best? The short answer is that it depends. Although the central theorem of welfare economics constitutes a powerful argument in favor of the market, it is only a benchmark for thinking and is subject to many important exceptions and qualifications. Earlier in this chapter we discussed categories of problems with the functioning of the market: lack of consumer information, monopoly, externalities, and public goods. In each of these cases, intervention in the market may advance social welfare.

Another point should be mentioned that we haven't remarked upon: use of the market involves transaction costs of various types, and in some domains it may be better to avoid them with other regimes. One important example is the vast amount of activity that takes place *within* firms and other organizations. Typically, this activity takes place because of commands and orders, not through the medium of a market. When an employee performs a

---

14. The argument that policies should be evaluated solely on efficiency grounds and that redistribution should be pursued through the income tax system is sometimes thought not to hold because the income tax may result in dilution of incentives to work. To illustrate: It might be asserted that drug prices should be controlled to help the poor, because using the tax system to help them would further reduce their incentive to work. This line of argument is fallacious, however, because controlling drug prices would also dilute the incentive to work. Space doesn't allow the matter to be pursued further here, except for reiteration of a point: the conclusion remains that, even when the influence of the income tax on work effort is recognized, it is still best to choose policies *only* on the basis of their effect on efficiency and to pursue distributional objectives only through the income tax.

particular task, it isn't because he or she is paid something for doing that task; rather, it's because this is what was ordered; when one division of a company produces a part of a machine and supplies it to another division of the company for further work, it is generally not paid to make the transfer but is, rather, working according to overall production plans. The reason that all this activity occurs without the market mediating it has to do with the simplicity of using orders, especially when the party issuing the orders has the information needed to determine the proper action. Economists are actively studying the functioning of organizations, and the theme of their work is hardly that a mini-market, a market in the small, should guide the activity that is observed. It is, rather, that the market is not the best way to undertake this activity.

4. Does economics leave out soft variables, hard-to-measure things, and thus overlook important factors? There is no principle of economics that would lead to exclusion of any factor that matters to individuals. Practitioners of economics, however, might have a tendency to give short shrift to factors of importance if they are difficult to evaluate. For example, an economist evaluating a policy for preserving wilderness areas might fail to take into proper account subtle but important benefits of such preservation to our population (e.g., perhaps we would be made happier because our visits to wilderness areas or even our awareness of their continued existence enhances our ability to appreciate nature). Obviously, such a failure to include appropriately a relevant factor in a social welfare evaluation should not be considered an intrinsic drawback of welfare economics, but, rather, of how it might be applied.

5. Does economic thinking not give due weight to notions of fairness? The term *fairness* is used in multiple senses. One sense in which it is employed concerns the fairness of the distribution of income. This aspect of fairness, we have already said, may be taken into account in a measure of social welfare. Notably, we emphasized that the measure may be such that social welfare is raised the more equal the distribution of income.[15] Thus, fairness in the *income distributional sense* is definitely accommodated within the framework of welfare economics.

Another very general category of use of the term fairness is that in many contexts, we have beliefs about proper outcomes and treatment of individuals. For instance, we have ideas of what proper punishment is for wrongdoing, of the circumstances in which we ought to honor contracts, of whether individuals in many situations should be benefitted or penalized, as the case may be, in a manner that is independent of their race or gender. These particularistic notions of fairness (which have no direct connection to the distribution of income or wealth) are many and varied, and they relate to welfare economics in several ways. First, individuals may care about the satisfaction of notions of fairness per se (a person may care whether punishment is in proportion to wrongdoing, about keeping contracts, about not discriminating). To this extent, individuals' utility, and thus social welfare, is affected by adherence to the notions of fairness. Second, satisfaction of the notions of fairness may lead to changes in behavior and outcomes that increase social welfare (if we punish in proportion to wrongdoing, we may often turn out to deter appropriately; if we usually honor contracts, we may promote trust and joint enterprise; if we do not discriminate, we may advance production and create beneficial incentives). Third, we may want to invest social resources in inculcating beliefs in notions of fairness (by parents, teachers, religious authorities), because such

---

15. There are two reasons why social welfare may increase if the distribution of income is made more nearly equal. (1) As mentioned already, equalizing incomes tends to make the utilities of different individuals more nearly equal, and social welfare may increase the more equal are peoples' utilities. (2) The marginal utility that individuals derive from income may fall the more income they have. If this is so, then shifting a dollar of income from rich to poor raises the poor person's utility by more than it lowers the rich person's utility. Hence, total utility tends to increase as a result of the redistribution, and thus social welfare often rises as well.

beliefs lead to increases in social welfare, as just noted. Hence, the connections between welfare economics and the study of morality and ethics are significant.[16]

---

16. The relationship between morality and social welfare was studied by economically oriented writers such as Bentham and Sidgwick in the nineteenth century, and is today undergoing a resurgence.

8. Suggestions for Further Reading

Two recommendations for an introductory treatment of microeconomics are N. Gregory Mankiw, *Principles of Economics*, 2nd ed. (Fort Worth, TX: Harcourt, 2001), and Michael Parkin, *Microeconomics*, 2nd ed. (Reading, MA: Addison-Wesley, 2000). A good intermediate text is Robert Pindyck and Daniel Rubinfeld, *Microeconomics*, 5th ed. (Upper Saddle River, NJ: Prentice-Hall, 2001).

Index